Buddhist Ethics: A Very Short Introduction

VERY SHORT INTRODUCTIONS are for anyone wanting a stimulating and accessible way in to a new subject. They are written by experts, and have been published in more than 25 languages worldwide.

The series began in 1995, and now represents a wide variety of topics in history, philosophy, religion, science, and the humanities. Over the next few years it will grow to a library of around 200 volumes – a Very Short Introduction to everything from ancient Egypt and Indian philosophy to conceptual art and cosmology.

Very Short Introductions available now:

THE RUSSIAN REVOLUTION
  S. A. Smith
SCHIZOPHRENIA
  Chris Frith and Eve Johnstone
SCHOPENHAUER
  Christopher Janaway
SHAKESPEARE   Germaine Greer
SOCIAL AND CULTURAL
  ANTHROPOLOGY
  John Monaghan and Peter Just
SOCIOLOGY   Steve Bruce
SOCRATES   C. C. W. Taylor

THE SPANISH CIVIL WAR
  Helen Graham
SPINOZA   Roger Scruton
STUART BRITAIN   John Morrill
TERRORISM
  Charles Townshend
THEOLOGY   David F. Ford
THE TUDORS   John Guy
TWENTIETH-CENTURY
  BRITAIN   Kenneth O. Morgan
WITTGENSTEIN   A. C. Grayling
WORLD MUSIC   Philip Bohlman

Available soon:

AFRICAN HISTORY
  John Parker and
  Richard Rathbone
THE BRAIN   Michael O'Shea
CHAOS   Leonard Smith
CITIZENSHIP   Richard Bellamy
CLASSICAL ARCHITECTURE
  Robert Tavernor
CONTEMPORARY ART
  Julian Stallabrass
THE CRUSADES
  Christopher Tyerman
THE DEAD SEA SCROLLS
  Timothy Lim
DERRIDA   Simon Glendinning
ECONOMICS   Partha Dasgupta
THE END OF THE WORLD
  Bill McGuire
ELEMENTS   Philip Ball
EXISTENTIALISM   Thomas Flynn
FEMINISM   Margaret Walters
THE FIRST WORLD WAR
  Michael Howard
FOSSILS   Keith Thomson
FUNDAMENTALISM
  Malise Ruthven
HUMAN EVOLUTION
  Bernard Wood

INTERNATIONAL RELATIONS
  Paul Wilkinson
JAZZ   Brian Morton
JOURNALISM   Ian Hargreaves
MANDELA   Tom Lodge
THE MARQUIS DE SADE
  John Phillips
THE MIND   Martin Davies
NATIONALISM   Steven Grosby
PERCEPTION   Richard Gregory
PHILOSOPHY OF RELIGION
  Jack Copeland and Diane Proudfoot
PHOTOGRAPHY   Steve Edwards
RACISM   Ali Rattansi
THE RAJ   Denis Judd
THE RENAISSANCE   Jerry Brotton
ROMAN EMPIRE
  Christopher Kelly
SARTRE   Christina Howells
SIKHISM   Eleanor Nesbitt
SOCIALISM   Michael Newman
A HISTORY OF TIME
  Leofranc Holford-Strevens
TRAGEDY   Adrian Poole
THE VIKINGS   Julian Richards
THE WORLD TRADE
  ORGANIZATION
  Amrita Narlikar

For more information visit our web site

www.oup.co.uk/vsi/

Damien Keown

BUDDHIST
ETHICS

A Very Short Introduction

OXFORD
UNIVERSITY PRESS

OXFORD

UNIVERSITY PRESS

Great Clarendon Street, Oxford OX2 6DP

Oxford University Press is a department of the University of Oxford.
It furthers the University's objective of excellence in research, scholarship,
and education by publishing worldwide in

Oxford New York

Auckland Cape Town Dar es Salaam Hong Kong Karachi
Kuala Lumpur Madrid Melbourne Mexico City Nairobi
New Delhi Shanghai Taipei Toronto

With offices in

Argentina Austria Brazil Chile Czech Republic France Greece
Guatemala Hungary Italy Japan Poland Portugal Singapore
South Korea Switzerland Thailand Turkey Ukraine Vietnam

Oxford is a registered trade mark of Oxford University Press
in the UK and in certain other countries

Published in the United States
by Oxford University Press Inc., New York

© Damien Keown 2005

The moral rights of the author have been asserted

Database right Oxford University Press (maker)

First published as a Very Short Introduction 2005

British Library Cataloguing in Publication Data

Data available

Library of Congress Cataloging in Publication Data

Data available

ISBN 0-19-280457-X

1 3 5 7 9 10 8 6 4 2

Typeset by RefineCatch Ltd, Bungay, Suffolk
Printed in Great Britain by
TJ International Ltd., Padstow, Cornwall

Contents

Preface

This book is written for a broad general readership. It is for Buddhists interested in ethical questions, for ethicists interested in Buddhism, for school or university students exploring the ethics of Buddhism – perhaps in conjunction with other world religions – and for the general reader who is simply curious about whether an Eastern tradition such as Buddhism can shed any light on problems that the West has found difficult and divisive.

The book offers an overview of how Buddhism might respond to the ethical dilemmas confronting the modern world. It discusses six contemporary issues: animals and the environment, sexuality, war and terrorism, abortion, suicide and euthanasia, and cloning. As a preliminary to addressing these topics, the first chapter explains the basic moral teachings of Buddhism and the second considers theoretical questions about the nature of these teachings in relation to Western ethics. Since Buddhist ethics is an unfamiliar subject in the West, a strategy adopted in some chapters is to take the more familiar Christian perspective on the issues as a point of departure. This allows comparisons and contrasts to be drawn with Buddhism, and hopefully will accelerate the reader's grasp of what is distinctive in the Buddhist approach.

As its name implies, the discipline of Buddhist ethics emerges from the interface between two complex and largely independent fields of knowledge – Buddhism and ethics. Separate introductions to both of these disciplines are available in the present series, and this short work makes no attempt to replace them. Instead, its aim is to focus on the point where these subjects intersect to form a new field of enquiry, one that has so far received very little attention from experts in either of its component disciplines.

A basic knowledge of Buddhism is assumed in the pages that follow, and readers who lack this are advised to consult first my companion volume in the series *Buddhism: A Very Short Introduction.* Some material relating to ethics there has been adapted for use here, notably the explanation of karma in Chapter 1, but the discussion of basic doctrines such as the Four Noble Truths has not been repeated. The 'Buddhism' discussed in the present work is not that of any one school, culture, or historical period, and, although my own expertise is in Theravāda Buddhism, my remarks are made with respect to an amorphous fiction which for convenience might be termed 'mainstream Buddhism'. What is meant by this is explained further in Chapter 2. While endeavouring to represent the views of the mainstream, however, this work has no pretensions to being authoritative or definitive. It scarcely needs saying that the issues explored here are controversial, and while some readers may find that the approach taken is congenial to their own reading of Buddhism, others will no doubt disagree, perhaps strongly, with the conclusions reached. Disagreements on ethical matters are almost inevitable given the nature of the subject matter, but hopefully even readers who disagree will feel better informed about alternative perspectives. Overall, I have tried to adopt the role of sympathetic critic, identifying what I see as both the strengths and weaknesses of the Buddhist perspective in the hope of generating a productive dialogue.

The task of writing this short book has been greatly assisted by the publication of Peter Harvey's longer introductory work *An Introduction to Buddhist Ethics: Foundations, Values and Issues* (Cambridge: Cambridge University Press, 2000). This excellent textbook contextualizes the issues with more historical, cultural, and textual detail than can be included in the present volume, and is recommended to readers who wish to pursue the subject at greater length. The Further reading section at the end of this volume contains additional guidance on sources relating to the particular topics discussed herein.

Acknowledgements

This book is based on a course taught at Goldsmiths College, London, and I am grateful to present and past students for their interest in the subject and their questions and comments over the years. I am grateful to Goldsmiths College and to the Arts and Humanities Research Board for funding sabbatical leave to allow me to complete the book during the academic year 2003–4, and to the publishers for permission to reuse some material mainly from Chapters 2 and 8 of my companion volume in the series, *Buddhism: A Very Short Introduction*. I am also indebted to my former student Pragati Sahni for her assistance with Chapter 3. Finally, I would like to thank George Miller for inaugurating this project during his time with the Press, and Emma Simmons and Marsha Filion for seeing the volume through to publication.

Note on citations and pronunciation

From time to time, the reader will encounter references in the form D.ii.95. These are references to Buddhist scriptures, specifically the Pāli Text Society editions of the Theravāda Buddhist canon. The key to the reference is as follows. The initial letter refers to one of the five divisions (*nikāyas*) into which the Buddha's discourses (*suttas*) are collated.

D   Dīgha Nikāya
M   Majjhima Nikāya
A   Aṅguttara Nikāya
S   Saṃyutta Nikāya
K   Khuddaka Nikāya

The Roman numeral (ii) denotes the volume number, and the Arabic numeral (95) denotes the page number. Thus the reference D.ii.95 is to volume two, page 95, of the Dīgha Nikāya.

A small number of references with the prefix Vin will also be encountered. These refer to a division of the Pāli canon known as the Vinaya, which contains material relating to monastic law. Independent texts from the Khuddaka Nikāya, such as the *Sutta Nipāta*, also have their own abbreviations (in this case Sn). A capital letter A after any of the above abbreviations (such as DA) means the reference is to the commentary (*aṭṭhakathā*) on the text in question. Translations of the entire Pāli canon into English have been published by the

Pāli Text Society (http://www.palitext.demon.co.uk/) and more recent translations are available from Wisdom Publications (http://www.wisdompubs.org). Translations of other texts cited are mentioned in Further Reading.

Language and pronunciation

Buddhist texts were composed in and translated into many languages, including Pāli, Sanskrit, Tibetan, Thai, Burmese, Chinese, Japanese, and Korean. The convention followed here is to cite Buddhist technical terms in their Sanskrit forms except when the discussion refers to Pāli sources at which time Pāli forms are used. Transliteration from languages such as Sanskrit and Pāli requires the use of diacritics. This is because the 26 letters of the English alphabet are insufficient to represent the larger number of characters in Asian languages. A horizontal line (macron) above a vowel lengthens it, such that the character 'a' is pronounced as in 'far' rather than 'fat'. For the most part, the other marks do not affect pronunciation sufficiently to be of any concern, with the following exceptions:

> c pronounced 'ch' as in 'choose'
> ṣ or ś pronounced 'sh' as in 'shoes'
> ñ pronounced 'ny' as in Spanish 'mañana'

A dot beneath a consonant (ṭ, ḍ, etc.) indicates that the tongue touches the roof of the mouth when pronouncing these letters, to give the characteristic sound of English when spoken with an Indian accent.

List of illustrations

1. Buddhism in Asia

Chapter 1
Buddhist morality

Morality is woven into the fabric of Buddhist teachings and there is no major branch or school of Buddhism that fails to emphasize the importance of the moral life. The scriptures of Buddhism in every language speak eloquently of virtues such as non-violence and compassion, and the Buddhist version of the 'Golden Rule' counsels us not to do anything to others we would not like done to ourselves. Although newcomers to Buddhism are often struck by the variety of the different Asian traditions, as divergent in form as Zen and Tibetan Buddhism, at the level of moral teachings there is much common ground. Some might disagree, but my own view is that we can speak of a common moral core underlying the divergent customs, practices, and philosophical teachings of the different schools. This core is composed of the principles and precepts, and the values and virtues expounded by the Buddha in the 5th century BCE and which continue to guide the conduct of some 350 million Buddhists around the world today. The purpose of this first chapter is to review these basic moral teachings.

Dharma

The ultimate foundation for Buddhist ethics is Dharma. Dharma has many meanings, but the underlying notion is of a universal law which governs both the physical and moral order of the universe. Dharma can best be translated as 'natural law', a term that captures

The Four Noble Truths

Duḥkha – All existence is suffering.
Samudāya – Suffering is caused by craving.
Nirodha – Suffering can have an end.
Mārga – The way to the end of suffering is the Noble Eightfold Path.

both its main senses, namely as the principle of order and regularity seen in the behaviour of natural phenomena, and also the idea of a universal moral law whose requirements have been revealed by enlightened beings such as the Buddha (note that Buddha claimed only to have discovered Dharma, not to have invented it). Every aspect of life is regulated by Dharma, from the succession of the seasons to the movement of the planets and constellations. Dharma is neither caused by nor under the control of a supreme being, and the gods themselves are subject to its laws, as was the Buddha. In the moral order, Dharma is manifest in the law of karma, which, as we shall see below, governs the way moral deeds affect individuals in present and future lives. Living in accordance with Dharma and implementing its requirements is thought to lead to happiness, fulfilment, and salvation; neglecting or transgressing it is said to lead to endless suffering in the cycle of rebirth (*saṃsāra*).

In his first sermon, the Buddha was said to have 'turned the wheel of the Dharma' and given doctrinal expression to the truth about how things are in reality. It was in this discourse that the Buddha set out the Four Noble Truths, the last of which is the Noble Eightfold Path which leads to nirvana. The Path has three divisions – Morality (*śīla*), Meditation (*samādhi*), and Insight (*prajñā*) – from which it can be seen that morality is an integral component of the path to nirvana.

The Eightfold Path and its Three Divisions

1. **Right View**
2. **Right Resolve** } Insight (*prajñā*)

3. **Right Speech**
4. **Right Action** } Morality (*śīla*)
5. **Right Livelihood**

6. **Right Effort**
7. **Right Mindfulness** } Meditation (*samādhi*)
8. **Right Meditation**

Karma

The doctrine of karma is concerned with the ethical implications of Dharma, in particular those relating to the consequences of moral behaviour. Karma is not a system of rewards and punishments meted out by God but a kind of natural law akin to the law of gravity. In popular usage in the West, karma is thought of simply as the good and bad things that happen to a person, a little like good and bad luck. However, this oversimplifies what for Buddhists is a complex of interrelated ideas which embraces both ethics and belief in reincarnation. The literal meaning of the Sanskrit word karma is 'action', but karma as a religious concept is concerned not with just any actions but with actions of a particular kind. Karmic actions are moral actions, and the Buddha defined karma by reference to moral choices and the acts consequent upon them. He stated, 'It is intention (*cetanā*), O monks, that I call karma; having willed one acts through body, speech, or mind' (A.iii.415).

Moral actions are unlike other actions in that they have both transitive and intransitive effects. The transitive effect is seen in the direct impact moral actions have on others; for example, when we kill or steal, someone is deprived of his life or property. The intransitive effect is seen in the way moral actions affect the agent. According to Buddhism, human beings have free will, and in the exercise of free choice they engage in self-determination. In a very real sense, individuals create themselves through their moral choices. By freely and repeatedly choosing certain sorts of things, individuals shape their characters, and through their characters their futures. As the English proverb has it: 'Sow an act, reap a habit; sow a habit, reap a character; sow a character, reap a destiny.' The process of creating karma may be likened to the work of a potter who moulds the clay into a finished shape: the soft clay is one's character, and when we make moral choices we hold ourselves in our hands and shape our natures for good or ill. It is not hard to see how even within the course of a single lifetime particular patterns of behaviour lead inexorably to certain results. Great works of literature reveal how the fate that befalls the protagonists is due not to chance but to a character flaw that leads to a tragic series of events. The remote effects of karmic choices are referred to as the 'maturation' (*vipāka*) or 'fruit' (*phala*) of the karmic act. The metaphor is an agricultural one: performing good and bad deeds is like planting seeds that will fruit at a later date. Othello's jealousy, Macbeth's ruthless ambition, and Hamlet's hesitation and self-doubt would all be seen by Buddhists as karmic seeds, and the tragic outcome in each case would be the inevitable 'fruit' of the choices these character-traits predisposed the individual to make. Individuals are thus to a large extent the authors of their good and bad fortune.

Not all the consequences of what a person does are experienced in the lifetime in which the deeds are performed. Karma that has been accumulated but not yet experienced is carried forward to the next life, or even many lifetimes ahead. Certain key aspects of a person's next rebirth are thought of as karmically determined. These include the family into which one is born, one's social status, physical appearance, and of course, one's character and personality, since these are simply carried over from the previous life. The doctrine of karma, however, does not claim that everything that happens to a person is karmically determined. Many of the things that happen in life – like winning a raffle or catching a cold – may simply be random events or accidents. Karma does not determine precisely what will happen or how anyone will react to what happens, and individuals are always free to resist previous conditioning and establish new patterns of behaviour.

What, then, makes an action good or bad? From the Buddha's definition above, it can be seen to be largely a matter of intention and choice. The psychological springs of motivation are described in Buddhism as 'roots', and there are said to be three good roots and three bad roots. Actions motivated by greed (*rāga*), hatred (*dveṣa*), and delusion (*moha*) are bad (*akuśala*), while actions motivated by their opposites – non-attachment, benevolence, and understanding – are good (*kuśala*). Making progress to enlightenment, however, is not simply a matter of having good intentions, and evil is sometimes done by people who act from the highest motives. Good intentions, therefore, must find expression in right actions, and right actions are basically those that are wholesome and do no harm to either oneself or others. The kinds of actions that fail these requirements are prohibited in various sets of precepts, about which more will be said below.

Merit

Karma can be either good or bad. Buddhists speak of good karma as 'merit' (*puṇya*; Pāli, *puñña*), and much effort is expended in acquiring it (its opposite, bad karma, is known as *pāpa*). Some Buddhists picture merit as a kind of spiritual capital – like money in a bank account – whereby credit is built up as the deposit on a heavenly rebirth. One of the best ways for a layman to earn merit is by supporting the *sangha*, or order of monks. This can be done by placing food in the bowls of monks as they pass on their daily alms round, by providing robes for the monks, by listening to sermons and attending religious services, and by donating funds for the upkeep of monasteries and temples. Merit can even be made by congratulating other donors and rejoicing in their generosity. Some Buddhists make the accumulation of merit an end in itself, and go to the extreme of carrying a notebook to keep a tally of their karmic 'balance'. This is to lose sight of the fact that merit is earned as a by-product of doing what is right. To do good deeds simply to obtain good karma would be to act from a selfish motive, and would not earn much merit.

In many Buddhist cultures, there is a belief in 'merit transference', or the idea that good karma can be shared with others, just like money. Donating good karma has the happy result that instead of one's own karmic balance being depleted, as it would in the case of money, it increases as a result of the generous motivation in sharing. The more one gives, the more one receives! It is doubtful to what extent there is canonical authority for notions of this kind, although the motivation to share one's merit in a spirit of generosity is certainly karmically wholesome since it would lead to the formation of a generous and benevolent character.

Precepts

In common with Indian tradition as a whole, Buddhism expresses its ethical requirements in the form of duties rather than rights. These duties are thought of as implicit requirements of Dharma. The most general moral duties are those found in the Five Precepts, for example the duty to refrain from evil acts such as killing and stealing. On becoming a Buddhist, one formally 'takes' (or accepts) the precepts in a ritual context known as 'going for refuge', and the

The Five Precepts (*pañcaśīla*)

This is the most widely known list of precepts in Buddhism, comparable in influence to the Ten Commandments of Christianity. The Five Precepts are undertaken as voluntary commitments in the ceremony of 'going for refuge' when a person becomes a Buddhist.

They are as follows:

1. I undertake the precept to refrain from harming living creatures.
2. I undertake the precept to refrain from taking what has not been given.
3. I undertake the precept to refrain from sexual immorality.
4. I undertake the precept to refrain from speaking falsely.
5. I undertake the precept to refrain from taking intoxicants.

form of words used acknowledges the free and voluntary nature of the duty assumed.

Apart from the Five Precepts, various other lists of precepts are found, such as the Eight Precepts (*aṣṭāṅga-śīla*) and the Ten Precepts (*daśa-śīla*). These are commonly adopted as additional commitments on the twice-monthly holy days (*poṣadha*; Pāli, *uposatha*), and supplement the first four of the Five Precepts with additional restrictions such as the time when meals may be taken. Another set of precepts similar to the Ten Precepts is the Ten Good Paths of Action (*daśa-kuśala-karmapatha*). Precepts like these which apply to the laity are comparatively few in number compared to those observed by monks and nuns, as explained below.

Vinaya

A term often found paired with Dharma is Vinaya. Particularly in early sources, the compound 'Dharma-Vinaya' ('doctrine and discipline') is used to denote the whole body of Buddhist teachings and practice. Originally, the Buddhist monastic order (*sangha*) existed as just another sect within a broad community of wandering teachers and students known as *parivrājakas* or *śramaṇas*. From these simple beginnings evolved a complex code for the regulation of monastic life which eventually became formulated in a portion of the canon known as the Vinaya Piṭaka. The Vinaya Piṭaka also contains a large number of stories and biographical material relating to the Buddha, as well as a certain amount of historical matter regarding the *sangha*.

The *Prātimokṣa*

The purpose of the Vinaya is to regulate in detail life within the community of monks and nuns and also their relationship with the laity. In its final form the text is divided into three sections, the first of which contains the set of rules for monks and nuns known as the *Prātimokṣa* (Pāli, *Pātimokkha*). The *Prātimokṣa* is an inventory of offences organized into several categories according to the gravity of the offence. It embraces not only moral questions, such as lying and stealing, but also matters of dress, etiquette, and the general deportment of monks and nuns. Many scholars now agree that the *Prātimokṣa* seems to have undergone at least three stages of development: as a simple confession of faith recited by Buddhist monks and nuns at periodic intervals; as a bare monastic code ensuring proper monastic discipline; and as a monastic liturgy, representing a period of relatively high organization and structure within the *sangha*. This inventory of offences became formalized into a communally chanted liturgy known as the *Prātimokṣa-sūtra*, which is recited as a kind of public confession at the *poṣadha*, or fast-day ceremony, on the new and the full moon days each month.

The *Prātimokṣa*

The *Prātimokṣa* for monks contains the following eight classes of offence:

1. *Pārājika dharmas*: offences requiring expulsion from the *sangha*.
2. *Sanghāvaśeṣa dharmas*: offences involving temporary exclusion from the *sangha* while undergoing a probationary period.
3. *Aniyata dharmas*: undetermined cases (involving sexuality) in which the offender, when observed by a trustworthy female lay follower, may be charged under one of several categories of offences.
4. *Naiḥsargika-pāyantika dharmas*: offences requiring forfeiture and expiation.
5. *Pāyantika dharmas*: offences requiring simple expiation.
6. *Pratideśanīya dharmas*: offences that should be confessed.
7. *Śaikṣa dharmas*: rules concerning etiquette.
8. *Adhikaraṇa-śamatha dharmas*: legalistic procedures to be used in settling disputes.

The nuns' text contains only seven categories, the third being excluded. The total number of rules cited varies in the texts of the different Buddhist schools, ranging from 218 to 263 for the monks and from 279 to 380 for the nuns.

Virtues

Although the precepts, whether lay or monastic, are of great importance, there is more to the Buddhist moral life than following rules. Rules must not only be followed, but followed for the right reasons and with the correct motivation. It is here that the role of the virtues becomes important, and Buddhist morality as a whole may be likened to a coin with two faces: on one side are the precepts and on the other the virtues. The precepts, in fact, may be thought of simply as a list of things a virtuous person would never do.

Early sources emphasize the importance of cultivating correct dispositions and habits so that moral conduct becomes the natural and spontaneous manifestation of internalized and properly integrated beliefs and values, rather than simple conformity to external rules. Many formulations of the precepts make this clear. Of someone who follows the first precept it is said, 'Laying aside the stick and the sword he dwells compassionate and kind to all living creatures' (D.i.4). Abstention from taking life is therefore ideally the result of a compassionate identification with living things, rather than a constraint imposed contrary to natural inclination. To observe the first precept perfectly requires a profound understanding of the relationship between living beings (according to Buddhism, in the long cycle of reincarnation we have all been each others' fathers, mothers, sons, and so forth) coupled with an unswerving disposition of universal benevolence and compassion. Although few have perfected these capacities, in respecting the precepts they habituate themselves to the conduct of one who has, and in so doing come a step closer to enlightenment.

The task of the virtues is to counteract negative dispositions called *kleśas* (known in the West as 'vices'). The lengthy lists of virtues and vices that appear in Buddhist commentarial literature are extrapolated from a key cluster of three 'cardinal virtues', non-attachment (*arāga*), benevolence (*adveṣa*), and understanding (*amoha*). These are the opposites of the three 'roots of evil', or 'three poisons', namely greed (*rāga*), hatred (*dveṣa*), and delusion (*moha*). Non-attachment means the absence of that selfish desire which taints behaviour by allocating a privileged status to one's own needs. Benevolence means an attitude of goodwill to all living creatures, and understanding means knowledge of Buddhist teachings such as the Four Noble Truths. While these are the three most basic Buddhist virtues, there are many others, one of the most important of which is compassion (*karuṇā*). Buddhist sources spend a great deal of time encouraging people to cultivate virtuous dispositions as a means of spiritual development, and some scholars feel that given this emphasis on the virtues Buddhist ethics is best classified as a form of 'virtue ethics', a suggestion we will consider further in the next chapter.

Dāna

One of the most important virtues for lay Buddhists in particular is *dāna*, which means 'giving', or generosity. The primary recipient of lay Buddhist generosity is the *sangha* – since monks and nuns possess nothing, they are entirely dependent upon the laity for support. The laity provides all the material needs of the monastic community, everything from food, robes, and medicine to the land and buildings which constitute the monastic residence. In the *kaṭhina* ceremony, which takes place following the annual rains retreat in countries where Theravāda Buddhism is practised, cotton cloth is supplied to the monks by the laity for the purpose of making robes. The relationship is not just one-way, for in return monks provide Dharma teachings to the laity, and the gift of the Dharma is said to be the highest of all gifts. At all levels of society – between family members, friends, and even strangers – generosity is widely practised in Buddhist countries and seen as an indication of spiritual development. This is because the generous person, as well as being free from egocentric thoughts and sensitive to the needs of others, finds it easier to practise renunciation and cultivate an attitude of detachment. The story of Prince Vessantara, the popular hero of the *Vessantara Jātaka*, is well known in South Asia. Vessantara gave away everything he owned, even down to his wife and children! Many Theravāda sources praise *dāna*, and Mahāyāna sources emphasize the extreme generosity of bodhisattvas, who are disposed to give away even parts of their bodies, or their lives, in order to aid others. As we shall see below, *dāna* is also the first of the 'Six Perfections' (*pāramitā*) of a bodhisattva.

Ahiṃsā

One of the most basic principles of Buddhist ethics, and one for which Buddhism is widely admired, is *ahiṃsā*. Although the term literally means 'non-harming' or 'non-violence', it embodies much more than these negative-sounding translations suggest. *Ahiṃsā* is not simply the *absence* of something, but is practised on the basis of a deeply positive feeling of respect for living beings, a moral position associated in the West with the terms 'respect for life' or the 'sanctity of life'. The principle of respect for life as understood in Western ethics holds that it is always morally wrong to intentionally cause harm or injury to living creatures (some proponents of the principle allow exceptions in cases such as self-defence, but others do not). In India, the concept of *ahiṃsā* seems to have originated among the unorthodox renouncer (*śramaṇa*) movements, in other words among non-Brahmanical schools like Buddhism and Jainism. These placed greater emphasis on concern (*dayā*) and sympathy (*anukampā*) for living creatures, and an increasing empathy with them based on the awareness that others dislike pain and death just as much as oneself. Animal sacrifice, which had played an important part in religious rites in India from ancient times, was rejected by both Buddhism and Jainism as cruel and barbaric. Due in part to their influence, blood sacrifices in the orthodox Brahmanical tradition came increasingly to be replaced by symbolic offerings such as vegetables, fruit, and milk. Many Buddhists – especially followers of the Mahāyāna in East Asia – have embraced vegetarianism, since this diet does not involve the slaughter of animals (vegetarianism is discussed further in Chapter 3).

Among the renouncers, the principle of respect for life was sometimes taken to extremes. Jain monks, for example, took the greatest precautions against destroying tiny forms of life such as insects, even unintentionally. Their practices had some influence on Buddhism; for example, Buddhist monks often used a strainer to make sure they did not destroy small creatures in their drinking-water. They also avoided travel during the monsoon so they would not tread on insects and other small creatures that became abundant after the rains. Concern is even apparent in early sources about the practice of agriculture because of the inevitable destruction of life caused by ploughing the earth. In general, however, Buddhism regards the destruction of life as morally wrong only when it is caused intentionally (in other words, when the death of creatures is the outcome sought).

Due to its association with *ahiṃsā*, Buddhism is generally perceived as non-violent and peace-loving, an impression that is to a large extent correct. While Buddhist countries have not been free from war and conflict, as we shall see in Chapter 5, Buddhist teachings constantly praise non-violence and express disapproval of killing or causing injury to living things.

Compassion

Compassion (*karuṇā*) is a virtue that is of importance in all schools of Buddhism but it is particularly emphasized by the Mahāyāna. In early Buddhism, *karuṇā* figures as the second of the four *Brahma-vihāras*, or 'Divine Abidings'. These are states of mind cultivated especially through the practice of meditation. The four are loving-kindness (*mettā*), compassion (*karuṇā*), sympathetic joy (*muditā*), and equanimity (*upekkhā*). The practice of the four *Brahma-vihāras* involves radiating outwards the positive qualities associated with each, directing them first towards oneself, then to one's family, the local community, and eventually to all beings in the universe. In Mahāyāna iconography and art, the symbolic embodiment of compassion is the great bodhisattva Avalokiteśvara, 'the one who looks down from on high'. He is portrayed as having a

2. The Bodhisattva Avalokiteśvara, the embodiment of compassion, with a thousand arms and multiple heads and faces

thousand arms extended in all directions to minister to those in need and is constantly appealed to by those in difficult circumstances. In the course of time in Buddhism there appeared a doctrine of salvation by faith according to which the mere invocation of the name of a Buddha was sufficient, given the extent of the Buddha's compassion, to ensure rebirth in a 'Pure Land', or heaven.

Mahāyāna morality

The Mahāyāna was a major movement in the history of Buddhism embracing many schools in a sweeping reinterpretation of fundamental religious ideals, beliefs, and values. Although there is no evidence for the existence of the Mahāyāna prior to the 2nd century CE, it can be assumed that the movement began to crystallize earlier, incorporating the teachings of various existing schools. In the Mahāyāna, the bodhisattva who devotes himself to the service of others becomes the new paradigm for religious practice, as opposed to the *arhat*, or saint in the early tradition, who is now criticized for leading a cloistered life devoted to the self-interested pursuit of liberation. Schools that embraced the earlier ideal are henceforth referred to disparagingly as the Hīnayāna ('Small Vehicle'), or the Śrāvakayāna ('Vehicle of the Hearers'). In the Mahāyāna great emphasis is placed on the twin values of compassion (*karuṇā*) and insight (*prajñā*), and the bodhisattva practises six special virtues known as the 'Six Perfections' (*pāramitā*). It can be seen that three of these (*śīla*, *samādhi*, and *prajñā*) coincide with the three divisions of the Eightfold Path of early Buddhism, demonstrating both continuity and reconfiguration in the evolving moral tradition.

The Mahāyāna did not reject the ethical teachings of early Buddhism but subsumed them under an expanded framework of its

---

The Six Perfections (*pāramitā*)

Generosity (*dāna*)
Morality (*śīla*)
Patience (*kṣānti*)
Perseverance (*vīrya*)
Meditation (*samādhi*)
Insight (*prajñā*)

---

own, within which three levels were identified. The first level was known as 'Moral Discipline' (*saṃvara-śīla*) and consisted of the scrupulous observance of the moral precepts. The second level was known as the 'Cultivation of Virtue' (*kuśala-dharma-saṃgrāhaka-śīla*) and was concerned with the accumulation of the good qualities necessary for the attainment of nirvana. The third category was known as 'Altruistic Conduct' (*sattva-artha-kriyā-śīla*) and consisted of moral action directed to the needs of others. The Mahāyāna claimed that the early followers had access only to the first level and that their moral practices were deficient in lacking concern for the wellbeing of others.

The Mahāyāna is not a monolithic system, and there is no one 'official' code of ethics for either laymen or monks. The Vinayas of the early schools were not rejected and continued to be observed by monks and nuns alongside the new teachings recommended for bodhisattvas in Mahāyāna literature.

Skilful Means (*upāya-kauśalya*)

An important innovation in Mahāyāna ethics was the doctrine of Skilful Means (*upāya-kauśalya*). The roots of this notion are found in the Buddha's skill in teaching the Dharma, demonstrated in his ability to adapt his message to the context in which it was delivered. For example, when talking to Brahmins, the Buddha would often explain his teachings by reference to their rituals and traditions, leading his audience step by step to see the truth of a Buddhist tenet. Parables, metaphors, and similes formed an important part of his teaching repertoire, skilfully tailored to suit the level of his audience. The Mahāyāna developed this idea in a radical way by intimating, in texts such as the *Lotus Sūtra* (circa 1st century CE), that the early teachings were not just skilfully delivered, but were a means to an end in their entirety in the sense that they contained nothing that could not be modified to suit the demands of changing situations. This idea has certain implications for ethics. If the teachings the Buddha had given were provisional rather than ultimate, then perhaps the precepts they contain could also be of a provisional rather than an ultimate nature? Thus the clear and strict rules encountered in the early sources which prohibit certain sorts of acts could be interpreted more in the way of guidelines rather than as ultimately binding. In particular, bodhisattvas, the new moral heroes of the Mahāyāna, could claim increased latitude and flexibility based on their recognition of the importance of compassion. A bodhisattva takes a vow to save all beings, and there is evidence in many texts of impatience with rules and regulations which seem to get in the way of a bodhisattva going about his salvific mission. The new imperative was to act in accordance with the spirit and not the letter of the precepts, and some sources go so far as to allow *karuṇā* to override other considerations, and even sanction immoral acts, if the bodhisattva sees that so doing would prevent or reduce suffering.

The pressure to bend or suspend the rules in the interests of compassion results in certain texts establishing new codes of conduct for bodhisattvas which sometimes allow the precepts to be broken. In some of these, such as the *Upāya-kauśalya-sūtra* (circa 1st century BCE), even killing is said to be justified to prevent someone committing a heinous crime and suffering karmic retribution in hell. Telling lies, abandoning celibacy, and other breaches of the precepts are also said to be permissible in exceptional circumstances. It is not always clear whether such behaviour is held up by the texts as normative and a model for imitation by others, or to make a point about the great compassion of bodhisattvas, who willingly accept the karmic consequences of breaking the precepts as the price of helping others.

In Tantric teachings, too, the precepts are sometimes set aside. Tantra, also known as the Vajrayāna ('Diamond Vehicle') or Mantrayāna ('Vehicle of Mantras'), is a form of Buddhism that developed in India in the 6th century CE and is characterized by antinomianism (the reversal of moral norms) and the use of magical techniques that aim to speed the practitioner to enlightenment in a single lifetime. One of the basic techniques of Tantra is to transmute negative mental energies into positive ones using a form of mystical alchemy which is believed to transform the whole personality. By liberating energy trapped at an instinctual level in emotions such as fear and lust, it was thought that practitioners could do the psychological equivalent of splitting the atom and use the energy produced to propel themselves rapidly to enlightenment. In certain forms of Tantra, such practices involved the deliberate and controlled reversal of moral norms and the breaking of taboos in order to help jolt the mind out of its conventional patterns of thought into a supposedly higher state of consciousness. Examples of such activities include drinking alcohol and sexual intercourse, both serious breaches of the monastic rules. While some practitioners understood such teachings and practices literally, however, others saw them as merely symbolic and simply useful subjects for meditation.

Conclusion

We might summarize the key points of this brief survey by saying that Buddhist moral teachings are thought to be grounded in the cosmic law of Dharma rather than commandments handed down by God. Buddhism holds that the requirements of this law have been revealed by enlightened teachers and can be understood by anyone who develops the necessary insight. In leading a moral life, a person becomes the embodiment of Dharma, and anyone who lives in this way and keeps the precepts can expect good karmic consequences, such as happiness in this life, a good rebirth in the next, and eventually the attainment of nirvana. Buddhist moral teachings emphasize self-discipline (especially for those who have chosen the life of a monk or nun), generosity (*dāna*), non-violence (*ahiṃsā*), and compassion (*karuṇā*). Mahāyāna Buddhism places a special emphasis on service to others, which at times has led to a conflict between compassion and keeping the precepts. While the notion of Skilful Means and Tantric teachings have both had some influence on Buddhist ethics, the mainstream view has remained that the precepts express requirements of Dharma that should not be contravened.

Chapter 2
Ethics East and West

The last chapter set out the basic moral teachings of Buddhism, and in this chapter we reflect on these from a theoretical perspective as a prelude to addressing specific applied issues in the remainder of the book. Questions to be considered here include how we should classify Buddhism as an ethical system, the extent to which it resembles or differs from Western ethics, and the methodological problems in drawing comparisons between East and West. Another important topic is the apparent absence of a tradition of philosophical ethics in Buddhism. The chapter concludes with a summary of the history of the study of Buddhist ethics in the West, an introduction to the contemporary activist movement known as 'engaged Buddhism', and some reflections on whether there can be a representative 'Buddhist view' on moral issues.

The classification of ethics

Ethics as it evolved in the West may be said to have three branches: i) descriptive ethics; ii) normative ethics; and iii) metaethics. Broadly speaking, the job of the first is to give an objective account of the moral prescriptions, norms, and values of a community or group and to show how action-guiding precepts and principles are applied in specific contexts. The second branch, normative ethics, proposes general rules and principles governing how we ought to act and tries to define the character and shape of the 'good life', or the life we should lead. It also aims to offer justification and validation for norms it seeks to establish. Finally, metaethics sees its task as providing conceptual clarification by analyzing the meaning of moral terms and characterizing the logical relations in moral arguments. It critically examines the logic of ethical legitimation and validation, and considers the overall question of the vindication of competing ethical systems.

Applying this classification to the present volume, in setting out the basic moral teachings of Buddhism the previous chapter was concerned mainly with descriptive ethics; the present chapter discusses questions that are broadly of a metaethical nature; and the remainder of the volume addresses problems in normative ethics. Since our focus will be primarily on the application of normative principles to particular issues (for example, abortion, euthanasia, ecology, and war), we could say that the primary concern of this book is *applied normative ethics*.

Theories of ethics

Three of the most influential theories of ethics in the West have been deontology, utilitarianism, and virtue ethics. Immanuel Kant (1724–1804) was one of the leading exponents of deontological ethics, an approach that emphasizes notions of duty and obligation and is characterized by looking backwards for justification. For example, a deontologist might suggest that the reason I am morally obliged to give £5 to Tom is because I promised to do so when I borrowed the money from him yesterday. My promise in the past thus gave rise to a moral obligation which I now have a duty to discharge. Deontological systems of ethics typically emphasize rules, commandments, and precepts, which impose obligations we have a duty to fulfil. By contrast, utilitarianism – a theory closely associated with Jeremy Bentham (1748–1832) and John Stuart Mill (1806–1873) – seeks justification in the future through the good consequences that are expected to flow from the performance of an act. Utilitarians would justify the repayment of my debt by pointing to the satisfaction it will give Tom to have his money returned, the benefit of the maintenance of our friendship, the advantage of being able to decently ask Tom for another loan if the need arises, and the general good to society as a whole which flows from people keeping promises and paying debts. They will weigh up these consequences against the disadvantages of not repaying the loan – such as the loss of friendship, confidence, and trust – and conclude that the former of these alternatives is preferable and hence the morally correct choice.

Virtue ethics offers something of a middle way between the other two and tends to look both to the past and future for justification. According to virtue ethics, of which Aristotle (384–322 BCE) was a leading exponent, what is of primary importance in ethics are neither pre-existing obligations nor pleasant outcomes, but the development of character so that a person becomes habitually and spontaneously good. Virtue ethics seeks a transformation of the personality through the development of correct habits over the course of time so that negative patterns of behaviour are gradually replaced with positive and beneficial ones. The way to act rightly, according to virtue ethics, is not simply to follow certain kinds of rules, nor seek pleasant consequences, but first and foremost to *be* or *become* a certain kind of person. As this transformation proceeds, the virtuous person may well find that his or her behaviour spontaneously comes increasingly into line with conventional moral norms. In virtue ethics, however, in contrast to deontology, these norms are internalized rather than externally imposed. With respect to the consequences of moral conduct, it will not infrequently turn out that a person who adopts a consistent plan of life and lives according to a consciously chosen and integrated set of values will be the happier for it. There is here a similarity with utilitarianism, which sees the moral life as geared to the production of happiness. Aristotle called the state of wellbeing that results from living rightly *eudaimonia*, a term often translated as 'happiness' but which really means something like 'thriving' or 'flourishing'. Virtue ethics thus proposes a path of self-transformation in which a person comes gradually to emulate certain ideal standards of behaviour disclosed in the conduct of teachers or sages who have progressed further towards the goal of human fulfilment. The behaviour of these role models provides a template on which to shape our own conduct: their positive qualities reveal the virtues we should emulate, and the actions they systematically avoid become codified in the form of precepts that serve to guide their followers.

Comparative ethics

Can any of the three theories just outlined help us understand the nature of Buddhist ethics? Before making comparisons, we must pause to reflect on the methodological problems that such comparisons raise. Is it legitimate simply to compare Western ethics with Eastern ethics in a straightforward way, or are there cultural, historical, and conceptual differences that might distort or invalidate such a comparison? It may be that the assumptions and presuppositions of Western thought are not compatible with those of Buddhism, and an insufficiently sensitive or nuanced comparison may simply force Buddhism into a Procrustean bed, resulting in the neglect of important aspects of its teachings simply because they have no Western analogue. One might wonder, for example, whether Buddhism fits the Western category of a 'religion', or how it should be classified. Problems of this kind have exercised the minds of scholars working in the nascent field of comparative ethics in the last few decades, but as yet there is no agreed methodology for undertaking a comparative study.

Despite the possible pitfalls in drawing comparisons between East and West, it seems important to make the attempt in order to gain some theoretical understanding of the structure of Buddhist ethics. It can be noted that scholars working in other branches of Buddhist philosophy have not hesitated to draw comparisons between Buddhist and Western thinkers and concepts. One difference is that in studying these branches of Buddhist thought, Western scholars were joining in a conversation among Buddhists themselves that had begun centuries ago. Where ethics is concerned, however, there is no ongoing discussion in which to participate, and the conversation is only just beginning.

Virtue ethics

With the above caveats entered, I think it fair to say that the growing consensus among scholars is that Buddhist ethics bears a greater resemblance to virtue ethics than any other Western theory. There are sufficient points in common to speak at least of a 'family resemblance' between the two systems. This is because Buddhism is first and foremost a path of self-transformation that seeks the elimination of negative states (vices) and their replacement by positive or wholesome ones (virtues). This is the way one becomes a Buddha. The transformation of the 'man in the street' into a Buddha comes about through the cultivation of particular virtues (paradigmatically wisdom and compassion) leading step by step to the goal of complete self-realization known as nirvana.

There are differences: virtue ethics as developed in the West does not involve a belief in reincarnation or rebirth. It may, however, be thought to teach a 'naturalized' theory of karma in which the good consequences of moral action become manifest in the present as opposed to in future lives. Virtue, as Aristotle pointed out, is its own reward, and the virtuous person (in the virtue ethics tradition this means a morally authentic and psychologically integrated agent, not someone who is merely sanctimonious or pious) can expect to lead a more fulfilled and rewarding life, thus reaping the good consequences of their virtue, so to speak, in real time.

Not all scholars would agree with the identification just made between Buddhism and virtue ethics. An alternative view, also worthy of serious consideration, is that Buddhist ethics cannot be accommodated entirely within any of the available Western theoretical models. We have already noticed that Buddhism has features in common with all the theories outlined so far. In common with deontology, Buddhism has rules and precepts that approach the status of moral absolutes. Early sources tirelessly repeat that certain acts, such as taking life, are not to be performed under any circumstances, and rules of this kind are typical of deontological ethics. We can note in passing that as evidence *against* a deontological reading, the point is often made that since the precepts are voluntarily assumed – unlike the commandments of Christianity – Buddhism does not *impose* moral obligations on anyone. However, this overlooks the fact that Dharmic obligations exist whether or not one formally acknowledges or accepts them: bad karma will follow a misdeed regardless of whether or not one has formally taken the precepts. It would appear, therefore, that there is a subsisting deontological obligation to live morally incumbent on us all.

Perhaps an even closer similarity exists between Buddhism and utilitarianism. After the fashion of utilitarianism, many scriptural sources advise Buddhists to reflect deeply on the consequences of their moral choices. According to utilitarianism, right acts are those which bear good consequences, and in Buddhism the doctrine of karma teaches that there is a close relationship between good deeds and future happiness.

The Mahāyāna doctrine of Skilful Means also has a utilitarian aspect since it seems to prioritize successful outcomes over respect for the precepts. When coupled with an emphasis on compassion, it may be thought to resemble the Christian utilitarianism hybrid known as 'situation ethics' promoted by Joseph Fletcher (1905–1991) in which the maximization of love in the world is taken as the only standard of right and wrong. But again, there are differences. While utilitarianism relies solely on consequences for moral justification, Buddhism also places great weight on intention (*cetanā*). Another difference is that whereas Buddhism teaches that acts have good consequences because they are good acts, utilitarianism holds that acts are good because they have good consequences. We will return to this point below.

The absence of 'ethics' in Buddhism

It would be helpful if we could ask Buddhists themselves for guidance on where their religion stands on questions of the kind raised above. However, there is a curious absence of authoritative opinion on these matters. Contemporary Buddhist groups rarely publish position papers and the great thinkers of the past left no legacy in the form of treatises on ethics. There is not even a word for 'ethics' in the early Indian texts – the closest approximation to it is *śīla*, often translated as 'morality' but closer in meaning to disciplined behaviour or self-restraint. In the course of Buddhist history there never arose a branch of learning concerned with the philosophical analysis of moral norms. But what of the sources cited in the previous chapter which speak of virtues and precepts – do these not have something to do with ethics? Indeed they do, but in the sense that as moral teachings they constitute the subject matter or raw data of ethics rather than ethics itself.

Perhaps this point can be explained by introducing a distinction that is sometimes made between 'ethics' and 'morality'. Sometimes the question is raised as to why we have two words in English – often used interchangeably – for what appears to be the same thing. The simple answer is that we have two words because one word derives from Greek and the other from Latin, but an alternative explanation seeks to give a special nuance to each term. In this respect, it is suggested that 'morality' is used to denote the standards or values of a society as they exist 'on the ground', so to speak, while 'ethics' refers to the critical analysis of those values by people such as philosophers. One could thus say that morality provides the raw data for the ethicist's deliberations. Whatever its merits, this distinction (which I would not wish to press too far) is useful because it allows us to postulate that while Buddhism has a good deal to say about morality, it has little to say about ethics. On the whole, there seems to be a remarkable lack of interest or curiosity about the concepts and principles that underlie Buddhist moral teachings. On very few occasions, for instance, do we see the Buddha moving to a discussion of theoretical questions about ethics, or responding to ethical and political conundrums of the kind put to Jesus by the Pharisees, such as whether it was right to pay taxes to the Romans (Matt 22:17).

One of the few early texts to explore moral dilemmas is *Milinda's Questions*, and it is interesting that although the bulk of the work was composed in Sri Lanka, the debate recorded in this text took place in a Greek-influenced part of northwest India between a Buddhist monk (Nāgasena) and a Greek king (Milinda). In this text, we see the possible beginnings of a line of ethical enquiry similar to the Socratic paradoxes in Plato's early dialogues. As an example of these, in the *Euthyphro*, Socrates asks whether certain things are good because God commands them, or whether God commands them because they are good. A Buddhist version of this problem might ask whether certain acts are good because they are rewarded by karma, or whether they are rewarded by karma because they are good. This question is fundamental to an understanding of Buddhist ethics because the answer 'yes' to the first part would mean that Buddhist ethics is utilitarian, while an affirmative answer to the second part means that it is deontological. Surprisingly, this question appears never to have occurred to Buddhist thinkers, and unfortunately was not one of the paradoxes posed by King Milinda in his discussion with Nāgasena. By comparison, if we look at Western literature of roughly the same period as the Pāli canon, we find authors like Plato and Aristotle not only exploring such dilemmas but also composing major treatises on ethics and politics. Plato's *Republic* is an extended treatment of three interwoven themes – politics, justice, and ethics – and many of Aristotle's major works, notably the *Nicomachean Ethics* and the *Politics*, focus on these subjects. However, there appears to be no treatise by any Buddhist author which compares with these works; it is as if these subjects simply do not feature in the classical canon of Buddhist learning.

Reasons for the absence of ethics

Why is there so little extant literature on ethics in Buddhism? Could it be that just as Americans play baseball and the English play cricket, different cultures simply have different interests and expertise? Or are there deeper reasons, having to do with the different cultural histories of East and West? As everyone knows, the Greeks invented democracy, and the discipline of political science arose to develop constitutions founded on ethical principles such as justice. Classical thinkers such as Aristotle saw politics and ethics as inextricably linked and understood that a just and fair society had to be founded on secure and philosophically well-grounded moral foundations. The concept of justice, however, is seldom – if ever – mentioned in Buddhist literature. Perhaps this is because Buddhism grew up under a system which the Greeks would have regarded as despotism. Republican tribes, like the Śākya to which the Buddha belonged, were rapidly being conquered and annexed by powerful monarchies, one of which – the kingdom of Magadha – eventually became supreme. This provided the political foundations for the Mauryan Empire, which the Buddhist ruler Aśoka would inherit a few centuries later. In such a context, in which power resides with kings and emperors rather than with citizens, the disciplines of politics and ethics are largely redundant. Since throughout its long history Buddhism has lived predominantly under non-democratic political systems, perhaps it is not surprising that we do not find ethics and politics enjoying a prestigious place in its curriculum.

Another possible reason Buddhism has shied away from such matters is that its original impetus came from being a renouncer movement that rejected social life and the systems of religious law governing it (as exemplified in the Hindu Dharmaśāstra tradition, for example). There may well be other reasons, but given our limited state of knowledge of the historical development of Buddhist ethical ideas, such suggestions must remain speculative.

Buddhist ethics in the West

It is only since Buddhism arrived in the West that a nascent discipline of Buddhist ethics has developed. The beginning of the discipline can conveniently be dated to 1964, when Winston King, referring to 'the almost total lack of contemporary material on Buddhist ethics in English', published his book *In the Hope of Nibbāna*. King specified an interest in six aspects of Theravāda ethics and raised general questions about the role of ethics in Buddhism. In the 1970s, a number of Sri Lankan scholars, notably Jayatilleke and Premasiri, began to pose more explicit theoretical questions. Adopting Western terminology, Jayatilleke asked, with reference to Buddhist ethics:

> Is it egotistic or altruistic? Is it relativistic or absolutistic? Is it objective or subjective? Is it deontological or teleological? Is it naturalistic or non-naturalistic?

The focus on Theravāda ethics continued with the publication in 1970 of the Venerable Hammalava Saddhatissa's descriptive work *Buddhist Ethics*, which has remained in print for over 30 years. During this time, only a small number of other books have appeared, despite an explosion of Western interest in Buddhism and a flood of publications on other aspects of Buddhist thought. There was no scholarly journal devoted to Buddhist ethics until the present author and Charles S. Prebish founded the online *Journal of Buddhist Ethics* in 1994.

Theoretical classifications

How might we respond to the questions about the theoretical nature of Buddhist ethics posed by Jayatilleke above? I have suggested that Buddhism belongs to the family of ethical theory known as 'virtue ethics', and if this is correct it goes some way towards helping us classify its ethical teachings in terms of Western categories. We might say that Buddhism is both *egotistic* and *altruistic* in the sense that it sees moral conduct as leading simultaneously to the good of oneself and others. It is *relativistic* in the sense that it includes scope for flexibility where appropriate, but not in the sense of holding that moral norms (as distinct from customs and etiquette) are merely a function of local cultural and historical circumstances. It is *absolutistic* in holding that certain things are always immoral (greed and hatred, for instance) and that certain things are always good (such as compassion and non-violence). On the question of *objectivity*, we saw in the previous chapter that as an aspect of Dharma, Buddhist ethical teachings are thought to be objectively true and in accordance with the nature of things. If Dharma exists in this sense as an objective moral law it suggests that through the use of reason individuals can ensure that the choices they make are objectively valid – that is to say that they reach the same conclusions as would an enlightened reasoner. We can add that in maintaining that the truth about right and wrong is objective and can be known through the proper use of intellectual faculties such as insight (*prajñā*), Buddhism would appear to be a *cognitive* ethical philosophy. This means it holds that moral truth can be discerned through reason, and that moral judgements are not merely subjective or a matter of personal taste, like a preference for red wine over white wine. Finally, we can conclude that Buddhist ethics is *naturalistic* (naturalist theories of ethics hold that an account can be given of moral conduct at the level of natural science). Buddhism holds there is a close connection between ethics and psychology, which is seen in the way moral conduct leads gradually to a transformation in the nature of the individual as little by little the virtuous person evolves into a Buddha.

Pinning on various labels does not mean that the task of Buddhist ethics is complete; instead, it generates further questions. For example, a critic may point out that in teaching that Dharma denotes both what *is* and what *ought to be*, Buddhism seems to commit what ethicists in the West call the 'naturalist fallacy' of deducing an 'ought' from an 'is'. It is said to be a logical fallacy to derive *moral* conclusions from a purely *factual* description of the

How should we classify Buddhist ethics?

Question	Answer
egotistic or altruistic?	both, since it seeks the good for oneself and others
relativistic or absolutistic?	mainly absolutistic
objective or subjective?	objective
deontological or teleological?	neither, a form of virtue ethics
naturalistic or non-naturalistic?	naturalistic
cognitive or non-cognitive?	cognitive

world. There are also other problems to face associated with virtue ethics in general, such as how to resolve conflicts between particular virtues and what to do when virtuous persons disagree. There is no space to enter into a discussion of these problems here, and they are simply mentioned as examples of the kinds of question that will come to the fore as the dialogue between Buddhist and Western ethics proceeds.

Engaged Buddhism

More or less coinciding with the birth of Buddhist ethics was the appearance of a related movement known as 'engaged Buddhism'. While Buddhist ethics is concerned with the specifics of individual conduct, engaged Buddhism focuses on larger questions of public policy such as social justice, poverty, politics, and the environment. Clearly, there is a connection between them, and it can be no coincidence that both these disciplines have arisen at roughly the same time as Buddhism encounters the West. Perhaps we can see

Buddhist ethics and engaged Buddhism as corresponding to two of the major branches of Western thought – ethics and politics – which for one reason or another never attained an autonomous status in the canon of Buddhist learning.

Engaged Buddhism has become so important in modern Buddhism worldwide that one Buddhist scholar has argued that it has become a new 'vehicle', joining the previously identified three vehicles of Buddhism (Hīnayāna, Mahāyāna, and Vajrayāna). This does not mean to say that Buddhism had never been socially active in its early history, but rather that it is often perceived to be individual and passive in its approach to human social problems. This viewpoint may have been promoted by the earliest Western scholars who, in the 19th century, tended to focus on Buddhist texts that seemed world-rejecting. By contrast, more than a century later, and utilizing not only Buddhist values, but also American and European forms of social protest and active social involvement, socially engaged Buddhists have employed boycotts, protest marches, letter-writing campaigns, and a host of other techniques to actively project Buddhist values into the contemporary debate about the global issues that concern everyone on the planet.

The promotion of engaged Buddhism owes much to the Vietnamese monk Thich Nhat Hanh, now mainly resident at Plum Village near Bordeaux in France. Thich Nhat Hanh coined the phrase 'socially engaged Buddhism' as a label for three Vietnamese ideas emphasizing awareness in daily life; social service; and social activism. This threefold emphasis not only establishes a connection with social, political, economic, and ecological issues, but also gives a sense of involving the ordinary lives of families, communities, and their interrelationships. In other words, while engaged Buddhism applies to human rights issues, non-violence and environmental concerns, it also has an impact on the lives of individual Buddhists living 'in the world'.

3. Thich Nhat Hanh, 1966

Four styles of Buddhist ethics

One modern writer on engaged Buddhism – Christopher Queen –
has suggested that there are four different 'styles' of Buddhist ethics.
The first is called 'The Ethics of Discipline', in which the conduct
caused by mental impurities fuelled by the 'three poisons' of greed,
hatred, and delusion are combated by observing the five precepts.
Here, the focus is on the individual Buddhist practitioner. Then
there is 'The Ethics of Virtue', in which the individual's relationship
comes more clearly into focus by engaging in such practices as the
Brahma-vihāras mentioned in the previous chapter, namely loving-
kindness, compassion, sympathetic joy, and equanimity. This marks

a shift from observing strict rules to following a more internally enforced ethical framework. Third, there is 'The Ethics of Altruism', in which service to others predominates. Finally, there is the comprehensive 'Ethics of Engagement', by which the three previous prescriptions for daily living are applied to the overall concern for a better society, and this means creating new social institutions and relationships. Such an approach involves, as Queen maintains, awareness, identification of the self and the world, and a profound call to action. (It will be seen that this fourfold model builds on the threefold classification of Mahāyāna ethics described in Chapter 1.) With such an expanded concept of morality in mind, a number of engaged Buddhist activists have worked to extend the traditional principles of morality into a carefully developed plan of Buddhist social ethics. Critical to the attempt is the notion of extending the traditional five vows of the laity in accordance with a supplementary series of fourteen precepts devised by Thich Nhat Hanh as part of the Tiep Hien Order, or 'Order of Interbeing', a community of activist-practitioners founded in 1964. In 2003, Thich Nhat Hanh and his community also released an updated version of the *Prātimokṣa* for modern times which includes prohibitions on monks playing electronic games and using karaoke players!

Can there be a 'Buddhist view?'

Given the absence of a theoretical background, the lack for the most part of any clear precedent for addressing moral issues, and the relative absence of position papers or policy statements from contemporary Buddhist sects and schools, there are clearly obstacles in the way of formulating a Buddhist perspective on contemporary issues. We cannot simply assume that there will be a single 'Buddhist view' on any problem: just as there are divisions among Christians on fundamental issues, we can expect to find Buddhists occupying diametrically opposed positions on many questions. No doubt some will have been introduced to particular perspectives by their spiritual teachers and may be unwilling to consider alternative points of view. Given the diversity within the

The fourteen precepts of the 'Order of Interbeing'

1. Do not be idolatrous about or bound to any doctrine, theory, or ideology, even a Buddhist one.
2. Do not think the knowledge you presently possess is changeless absolute truth.
3. Do not force others to adopt your views, whether by authority, threat, money, propaganda, or even education.
4. Do not avoid contact with suffering or close your eyes to suffering.
5. Do not accumulate wealth while millions remain hungry.
6. Do not maintain anger or hatred.
7. Do not lose yourself in distraction, inwardly or outwardly.
8. Do not utter words that can create discord or cause your community to split apart.
9. Do not say untruthful things for the sake of personal advantage or to impress people.
10. Do not use the Buddhist community for personal gain or profit, or transform your community into a political party.
11. Do not live with a vocation that is harmful to humans or nature.
12. Do not kill. Do not let others kill.
13. Possess nothing that should belong to others.
14. Do not mistreat your body.

tradition, how can we know which is the authentic voice of Buddhism? This is one horn of the dilemma. The other is that until we know what the Buddhist view *is* on any given question, how can we engage in dialogue with it?

If, despite the absence of any central ecclesiastical authority, we can speak of a 'Buddhist view' on moral issues, as I believe we can, I suggest it should be one that both represents the consensus among the majority of major schools and has a foundation in the scriptural tradition. To formulate this requirement more systematically, for a view to be described as the 'Buddhist view', with the implication that it is orthodox or widely held, we would expect to find:

1. authority for it in canonical sources;
2. support for it in non-canonical or commentarial literature;
3. the absence of contradictory evidence or counter-examples in these two groups of sources (this applies especially to matters on which there is little or no textual discussion);
4. evidence that the view is pan-Buddhist (it is held by a majority of Mahāyāna and non-Mahāyāna schools);
5. confirmation that the view has a broad cultural base;
6. evidence that the view has been held consistently over time.

The more of these points there are in favour of a view, the greater the case for regarding it as an authentic expression of Buddhist principles.

Conclusion

This chapter has suggested that we can legitimately make use of Western concepts to understand the nature of Buddhist ethics, and has proposed a working classification of Buddhism as a form of virtue ethics. It has pointed out the apparent absence of a branch of learning concerned with ethics in the philosophical canon of Buddhism, and attributed this to disparities in the cultural history of Asia and the West. It noted the modern origins of the discipline of Buddhist ethics and the movement known as engaged Buddhism, identified theoretical labels for Buddhist ethics, and proposed criteria for a 'Buddhist view' on ethical issues. It is clear that at a theoretical level many important questions remain, but at least we now have a tentative basis on which to apply the moral teachings of Buddhism set out in Chapter 1 to the six areas of applied ethics to be discussed in the remainder of the book.

Chapter 3
Animals and the environment

Buddhism is often seen as an 'eco-friendly' religion with an
expanded moral horizon encompassing not just human beings
but also animals and the environment. It is generally thought to
have a more 'enlightened' attitude to nature than Christianity,
which has traditionally taught that mankind is the divinely
appointed steward of creation holding authority over the natural
order. Writers such as historian Lynn White (himself a Christian)
see this belief as one of the underlying causes of the contemporary
ecological crisis, since it encourages the idea that nature exists
simply to serve human interests and is there to be exploited as
circumstances demand. Buddhism, by contrast, is perceived
as pursuing a path of harmonious integration with nature
and as fostering identification and mutual respect within the
natural world. Since, according to Buddhist teachings, human
beings can be reborn as animals, and vice versa, the Buddhist
world view suggests a much closer kinship between species
whereby different forms of life are interrelated in a
profound way.

A visitor to any Buddhist country will see many examples of
spontaneous kindness towards animals. A custom common
in many Buddhist countries is that of 'releasing life', a practice
whereby animals kept in captivity are released upon payment
of a small fee. Typically, small birds are set free from their

cages, and it is believed that merit is gained by the donor for this act of kindness. On a more theoretical level, the doctrine of dependent origination is interpreted by some as teaching that the entire cosmos has an underlying metaphysical unity in terms of which all phenomena are linked in a delicate and complex web of relationships. The image of 'Brahma's net' is often used to illustrate this concept, the net being a web of jewels which glisten and reflect one another in their many different facets.

While there may be some truth in the view that Buddhism is more benign in its attitude towards nature than Christianity, the idea that Buddhism is deeply in tune with 'green' values and a natural ally of the 'animal rights' and other activist movements requires qualification. There is no doubt that Buddhist literature contains many references to animals and the environment, but when the context of these references is examined they often turn out to have little in common with the modern conservationist agenda or concern to reduce animal suffering. Human beings remain the primary focus of Buddhist teachings and since the basic aim of Buddhism is to guide human beings from the darkness of suffering (*duḥkha*) to the light of liberation, this should come as no surprise. In adopting what is in many respects an anthropomorphic position (the view that value belongs to humans alone and nature is to be protected for their sake and no other), the Buddhist view of nature may not be as far removed from the Christian one as is sometimes thought.

Ethical attitudes and the place of animals

At first sight, Buddhist texts appear to support the view that all living creatures must be respected. The first precept has a direct bearing on the treatment of animals since it prescribes non-violence not just towards human beings but to '*pāṇa*', or 'creatures.' The *Sutta Nipāta* categorically states:

Let him neither kill, nor cause to be killed any living being, or let him approve of others killing, after having refrained from hurting all creatures, both those that are strong and those that tremble in the world.

(v.393)

The Buddha himself is portrayed as refraining from destroying life and even from causing injury to seeds and plants (D.i.4). It is often stated that enlightened beings 'show kindness and live with compassion for the welfare of all living beings' (A.i.211). Abstaining from violence is a requirement of the Eightfold Path under the headings of Right Action and Right Livelihood. Right Action is said to include abandoning the taking of life (D.ii.312) and Right Livelihood forbids certain professions such as trade in flesh and weapons (A.iii.208). A categorical ban is imposed on hunting, butchering, and other similar professions (M.i.343). All the above directives are clearly aimed towards the protection of animals.

Also influential in defining ethical attitudes towards the natural world are the four *Brahma-vihāras*, mentioned in Chapter 1. Referred to as the 'sublime attitudes', universal love (*mettā*), compassion (*karuṇā*), sympathetic joy (*muditā*), and equanimity (*upekkhā*) foster feelings that lead to the protection of the natural world and ensure its wellbeing. A truly compassionate and loving human being would find it hard to reconcile these sentiments with callous environmental damage and cruel blood sports pursued merely for the sake of enjoyment. Though it becomes clear in the reading of Buddhist texts that the sublime attitudes are primarily prescribed for the spiritual advancement of the practitioner (S.ii.264) rather than for the benefit of the environment, it is admitted in the texts themselves that their practice gradually pervades the whole world. Although the natural world is not the direct object of these practices, then, it is at least an indirect beneficiary. The Mahāyāna emphasis on the 'great compassion' (*mahā-karuṇā*) of bodhisattvas, and the Yogācāra notion of the 'embryonic Buddha' (*tathāgata-garbha*) which holds that the universal seed of Buddhahood is present in all living beings, including animals, further strengthen the ethical identification between self and others which is vital to ecological concern.

The Buddhist values of non-violence and compassion are clearly expressed in the Buddha's opposition to animal sacrifice. Animal sacrifices are severely criticized and alternative sacrifices using oil, butter, and molasses are praised (D.i.141). The Buddha, on hearing that a great sacrifice was being planned that would include the slaughter of several animals, stated that no great merit would be gained from such an action (S.i.75). Yet although evincing concern for their suffering, Buddhist sources show little interest in understanding the nature of animals. It is clear that they are held to suffer pain, but beyond that their status is ambiguous. Sometimes animal birth is praised (M.i.341), but most commonly it is denounced as brutal and lowly (M.iii.169). Not infrequently it is hinted that animals are moral beings that have the capacity to produce good and bad karma. However, Buddhist literary sources often misrepresent the true reality of animal life. In some texts animals are given characteristics they do not have, and their biological reality is made obscure. This can be seen in an example from the *Jātakas*. The purpose of the *Jātaka* folktales is to impart moral lessons to human beings in the manner of Aesop's fables, but since animals and the natural world figure prominently in them, these tales are often quoted to demonstrate Buddhism's ecological credentials. The *Anta Jātaka*, for instance, is a tale showing the evil of flattery and greed. It describes the actions of a crow and a jackal, depicting them as greedy beings that resort to deceitful flattery in order to gain food (J. 440–441). As a moral fable, the tale is quite acceptable, but the fact that animals are the main protagonists should not by itself be taken as evidence of Buddhist concern for animals. Quite the contrary, in fact, for in this case it universalizes the characteristics of greed and flattery as qualities shared by all members of the crow and jackal species. It categorically states in its accompanying verse that jackals are the lowest of all beasts and crows are the lowest of all birds. The anthropomorphic portrayal of these animals thus leads to a universal degradation of them that has little to do with ecological concern and may even undermine it. This random association of moral qualities with certain species shows that Buddhism has little curiosity or interest in the animals themselves and uses them merely as symbols to represent *human* attributes.

Plant life and wilderness

The nature of plant life in Buddhism is similarly opaque. It is difficult to state definitively whether early Buddhists believed plants and vegetation to be on a par with other beings that suffer, or whether they were considered to be non-sentient. One detailed list of precepts includes a rule that forbids causing injury to seeds and crops (D.i.5), and there are *Prātimokṣa* injunctions that prohibit damage to vegetation, classifying it as a form of life with a single sense-faculty (*eka-indriya jīva*) (Vin.iii.155). It is not clear, however, whether these rules have to do with ecology or with Buddhist monks living up to the expectations of the laity, who would certainly have compared them with their Jain rivals (the Jains are famous even today for their strict discipline). Elsewhere, bad karma is said to follow the cutting of a branch or tree that once gave fruit and shade (A.iii.369), and merit is promised to those who plant groves and parks (S.i.33). The great Buddhist emperor Aśoka (3rd century BCE) planted trees and also medicinal herbs. Furthermore, in popular belief trees and plants merited respect as the abode of deities. This, however, remains an ambiguous criterion for ecology, for it could imply that a tree uninhabited by a deity can be cut down. It also suggests an interest in the protection of deities (theocentric) rather than the protection of trees (ecocentric).

As for the wilderness that forms an important part of the ecological agenda today, Buddhism gives no specific injunctions for its conservation, although aesthetic references to wild nature are found. For instance, the natural beauty of the Gosinga-sāla forest grove near Vesālī, full of perfumed trees in bloom, is described as very pleasing to the eye on a moonlit night (M.i.212). Since aesthetic arguments are often evoked in environmental ethics in order to justify preserving the wild beauty of nature, Buddhist aesthetics can be likewise employed. At the same time, one has to be aware that Buddhist literature also contains contrasting descriptions of opulent surroundings in which trees and ponds made of gold and other precious material are glorified (D.iii.182). Such descriptions suggest that the beauty of civilization was valued just as much as the beauty of the wilderness.

The 'hermit strand'

One of the most effective arguments for preserving the wilderness lies in what has come to be known as the 'hermit strand' in Buddhism. Identified initially by Lambert Schmithausen, this strand has to do with the advice given to hermits to live in natural surroundings in order to pursue the path of liberation without distraction (for example M.i.274). The Buddha himself chose to dwell in forests in order to pursue spiritual ideals (D.iii.54), and the fact that the main events in his life – such as his birth, enlightenment, first sermon, and death – all took place under trees or in parks seems to associate him with natural environments. The Buddha left a palace to live in the forest, and if there were no wilderness the religious seeker would be unable to seek refuge from active life. This seems to be one reason why the wilderness ought to be preserved. The basis of the hermit strand, however, is once again anthropocentric, and anthropocentrism is generally berated in environmental literature.

Equality or hierarchy?

One of the most important questions that an ethics concerned with the natural world may ask has to do with which forms of life merit moral consideration. There is no clear Buddhist position on this issue, but the view that all beings are equal and consequently deserve equal moral consideration is not easy to establish on Buddhist principles. Instead, Buddhism seems to assume a hierarchical structure among the living creatures in the universe. In the Buddhist description of *saṃsāra*, six realms, or *gatis*, are enumerated. These are hell, the animal realm, the ghostly world, the titans, human beings, and the heavenly realm (D.iii.264). Often represented in the 'wheel of life' (*bhavacakra*), three of these realms (those below the centre line) are classified as 'unfortunate' and three (those above the line) as 'fortunate' (see Figure 4).

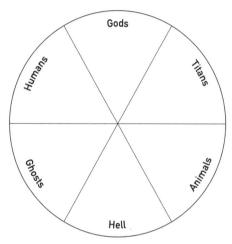

4. The wheel of life

Each of the six realms is accorded a separate status and nature, and there is a clear hierarchy among them. Animals occupy one realm and humans occupy another one, and it is clearly preferable to be born in the latter than the former. At the same time, there is a constant movement of beings within the different realms and no stage is permanent. It is worth noting, however, that a 'precious human rebirth' is given particular prestige, even greater than that of rebirth among the gods, for this is the most auspicious form of rebirth from which to attain liberation due to its special mix of happiness and suffering. However, even if humans have a unique value, it does not follow that *only* humans deserve moral consideration: a hierarchical structure suggests a graduated scheme of value rather than a purely anthropocentric one.

With respect to the animal world, a point of some interest is how far down the chain of being our moral obligations extend. The first precept, as mentioned earlier, prohibits causing injury to living creatures. This would include not harming or killing animals, but would it apply to insects and microscopic forms of life? The boundaries of the moral world are fuzzy at the lower echelons, and I have suggested elsewhere that the concept of 'karmic life' can provide a useful principle of demarcation. By 'karmic life' is meant those forms of life that are sentient, reincarnate, and are morally autonomous. This would include human beings and the higher mammals, but at the lower levels of the evolutionary scale there would be a significant number of species with an ambiguous moral status. Early texts say that humans may be reborn as scorpions and centipedes (A.v.289), or even worms and maggots (M.iii.168). Below this threshold, as in the case of microscopic forms of life such as viruses and bacteria, the obligations of the first precept would not apply, since these entities do not reincarnate and are simply functioning parts of an integral being rather than autonomous agents. A virus, for example, is not sentient (it lacks a central nervous system through which pain is experienced), it has no karmic history (it has not lived before), and, being merely part of an organic whole, is no more a moral agent than an arm or a leg. An implication of adopting the criterion of karmic life, however, is that the greater part of the natural world – especially inanimate nature such as mountains, rivers, and lakes – would lack inherent moral value, although retaining instrumental value to the extent that it provides support for karmic life.

Even though a natural hierarchy seems to exist, Buddhist literature does not make use of this structure to discuss matters such as species conservation or selective conservation, which are issues that must be dealt with in modern ecology. In other words, there is no detailed discussion about a hierarchy within the animal kingdom itself or among the plant and animal kingdoms. This makes it difficult to address questions concerning which species should be saved, and the relative value between them. Different types of species are scarcely identified, let alone ranked in terms of those which are more deserving of moral consideration. The commentator Buddhaghosa suggests at one point that the larger the animal, the greater the 'demerit' in killing it (MA.i.189). On this understanding, killing an elephant is a more serious offence than killing a fly on account of the greater effort required. However, this logic is not terribly helpful when applied to the natural world as a basis for selection of species, for sometimes it is more important to ensure the survival of endangered smaller species in the face of larger predators. It is noteworthy that in monastic law, killing *any* animal is a minor (*pāyantika*) offence, while killing a human being is a much more serious one (a *pārājika*).

The practice of conservation can also lead to a conflict with *ahiṃsā*. For example, would Buddhism approve of a conservation measure that required the culling of some animals, even if such killing were ultimately to preserve the balance of the natural world? The Mahāyāna answer to this might introduce the concept of skilful means (*upāya-kauśalya*). Skilful means allow precepts to be relaxed or broken to varying degrees by a bodhisattva when done selflessly and for the welfare and happiness of other beings. However, applying skilful means with reference to the environment is a complicated issue and raises prior questions of the kind identified above, particularly *why* the welfare of some species is to be considered more important than others.

Vegetarianism

Vegetarianism is an often-debated issue in environmental literature. Though vegetarianism is sometimes thought harmful to ecology by those who consider humans as biologically meat-eaters, or see meat-eating as an important practice to control certain animal populations, arguments in support of vegetarianism are more common. Two reasons are frequently mentioned in favour of vegetarianism. First, many see modern ways of meat acquisition as harmful to the balance of nature since animals that are being reared for their meat consume far greater resources than they yield. This renders the entire process uneconomic and wasteful. Second, animals suffer when they are killed. This is known as the 'humane' argument and its aim is to reduce and ultimately put an end to animal suffering.

Among early texts, the *Jīvaka Sutta* of the *Dīgha Nikāya* sheds some light on the question of vegetarianism, even though there are no specific injunctions affirming or prohibiting it. The *sutta* describes various actions that have to be performed in the slaughter of an animal and each of these steps is seen as an evil deed deserving of demerit. These steps include the orders to fetch the being that is to be slaughtered, the act of fetching the being, the order for the being to be slaughtered, the act of slaughtering the being (who suffers immense pain as a result), and the meat generated being served to a Buddha or disciple who eats it unknowingly. This elaborate discussion not only stresses that an animal is not to be killed in order to feed a monk, it also draws attention to the inhumane process of slaughter. Thus the text appears to promote the humane argument for vegetarianism. The suspicion that vegetarianism may have been a preferred choice is also confirmed by the belief in the superior nature of non-violence and compassion and the prohibition on the professions of hunters and butchers. It is important, at the same time, to note that in the *Jīvaka Sutta* the Buddha allowed monks to accept and eat the meat that was offered to them on their alms rounds if they had not seen, heard, or suspected that the animal was killed for their sake. The earliest sources depict the Buddha as following a non-vegetarian diet and even resisting an attempt to make vegetarianism compulsory for monks. Many take this as confirmation that the Buddha had no objection to meat-eating, but it may equally well have been the case that since meat-eating was a widespread and accepted practice in the Buddha's time, accepting meat in alms was allowed for practical purposes. By allowing meat to be taken as almsfood, the Buddha may also have wanted to encourage the growth of non-attachment as a means to spiritual development.

The Mahāyāna, however, categorically denounces the eating of meat. The eighth chapter of the *Laṅkāvatāra Sūtra* is a good example of the various reasons often cited in support of vegetarianism by the Mahāyāna. These include that meat-eating causes terror to living beings, acts as a hindrance to liberation, and causes personal distress, such as producing bad dreams. An appeal is also based on the cycle of transmigration, such that the animal to be slaughtered may have been one's mother, father, or other relative in another lifetime. Further, the dead animal, as with any other dead body, has an offensive odour. The *Sūtra* also discusses the example of a meat-eating king whose excessive fondness and greed for meat made him resort to cannibalism. As a result, he was alienated from his relatives, his friends, and his people, and eventually had to abdicate.

Animal experimentation

Vegetarianism is just one of a range of issues that concern the treatment of animals. Questions can also be raised about animal experimentation in scientific research and the practice of vivisection. Vivisection in recent times has come to symbolize unnecessary cruelty to animals and a disregard for their suffering. Since, as mentioned above, Buddhism is a champion of compassion and non-violence, cruel and painful animal experimentation would be unacceptable. But this issue is not as simple as it appears, especially if the value given to other species is not egalitarian but relative. Considerable suffering results in the process of domesticating elephants, yet Buddhist texts turn a blind eye to such practices, except for certain rare examples such as the *Dubbalakaṭṭha Jātaka* (J.i.414–416) in which, though the pain is acknowledged, no directive to stop it is issued. It appears, then, that causing suffering to animals for human gain is permissible. This suggests that experimenting on a beagle for the sake of finding a cure for a Buddha may also be acceptable for the same reason, particularly if the experiments do not cause pain.

Similar problems arise in the case of pest control. Would a farmer who uses insecticides and pesticides in order to raise a healthy crop be acting immorally given the relativity of value among humans and other species? Clearly it would be better if insecticides were not needed, but if their use produces a larger crop which feeds more human beings, one can see an argument for employing them. This kind of conflict arises in other situations, as when insects or vermin infest a dwelling. On a strict interpretation of Buddhist principles, it appears as if all killing is forbidden, but at the same time practices that cause harm to non-human life may be defensible when there is no non-violent alternative and the primary intent is not to destroy life but simply, say, to make one's house habitable.

Conclusion

The above discussion shows that it is not an easy matter to classify Buddhism simply as 'ecologically friendly'. Buddhist attitudes towards the natural world are complex and at times contradictory. On the one hand, references to plants and animals prove Buddhism's awareness of the world of nature. On the other, the importance given to human beings as well as the fact that ultimate value is given to the pursuit of liberation leaves a clear impression that the natural world has at best a secondary or instrumental value. When all is said and done, the aim of Buddhist teachings is not to redeem *saṃsāra* by restoring its ecological balance but to attain nirvana, or at least as a secondary goal, to pass from the human world to the relative security of a heavenly birth. The fact that the world is seen as inherently flawed and imperfect, and ultimately a disvalue, seems to cast a shadow over the prospects for a Buddhist ecology.

How does Buddhism compare with contemporary ecological movements such as 'deep ecology' and ecofeminism? Although they have points in common, it is unlikely that the Buddhist perspective would coincide entirely with either of these. In contrast to deep ecology's goal of 'self-identification', Buddhism does not teach or encourage identification with nature. It acknowledges in the principle of dependent origination that certain causes lead to certain consequences and that everything that exists is subject to this law. But this is not to claim there exists a connection between all things in the sense in which this is understood in deep ecology. Some East Asian schools of Buddhism (notably Kegon) come close to such a view, but this is not how the concept of dependent origination is interpreted in early or later mainstream Buddhist thought. The view that the whole of the cosmos is intrinsically valuable and pure (often expressed in the image of 'Brahma's net' referred to earlier) may even be problematic for ecology to the extent that it appears to place carbon dioxide gases and nuclear waste on a par with rivers and lakes. There are also differences with ecofeminism: not only does Buddhism not criticize (or even recognize) the concept of 'androcentricism' (the belief that it is the conduct of men rather than the conduct of all human beings that is responsible for the depleted state of the environment today), but it also contains many negative depictions of women and is in fact considered by some feminists to be misogynist.

Perhaps a better way of establishing a basis for ecology in Buddhism is to emphasize the ecological aspects of the ethical virtues which are undeniably a central element in Buddhist teachings. Virtues such as loving-kindness, compassion, non-violence, and wisdom promote ecological concern by their very nature. Even though such virtues were not originally taught for this reason, they do tend to promote an outlook and way of life that has much in common with the aims of the ecology movement. If so, it may be claimed that ecological concern is an implicit part of Buddhism's teachings and that by adhering to its ethical injunctions a person simultaneously lives in harmony with the environment. Such an approach provides only the beginning of Buddhist ecology, however, and does not resolve the hard choices presented by projects such as the building of dams that will provide electricity at the cost of destroying the natural habitat of plants and animals. The basis upon which Buddhism would construct a calculus to resolve such dilemmas has yet to be clarified.

Chapter 4
Sexuality

Sexuality is an area on which Buddhism and Christianity seem at first glance to differ greatly, but on closer inspection – as in the case of ecology – turn out to have more in common than might at first be supposed. Christianity is sometimes seen as having a 'hang-up' about sex and to be overly concerned with virginity and celibacy, whereas Buddhism is perceived to be more relaxed and less 'neurotic' about this subject. The erotic art of Tibet, now familiar in the West, and a plethora of popular books about Tantric sex only reinforce the impression that Buddhism has a more 'liberated' view of sexual ethics.

Westerners who turn to Buddhism in the hope of finding the endorsement of a hippy-like attitude to 'free love', however, are likely to be disappointed. Contrary to popular belief, Buddhism is generally conservative on sexual matters, and traditional Buddhist societies tend to be reserved and even prudish where sex is concerned. Most Buddhist monks would be embarrassed to discuss questions of sex and reproduction, especially with women, and although attitudes are slowly changing, such matters are generally taboo. The Vinaya (iii.130) contains a rule that forbids monks speaking to women about obscene or erotic matters, and it may be thought that a frank discussion of sexual issues is sailing close to the wind. Although Tantric schools have flourished on and off down the centuries, the erotic art they made use of was mainly a means of conveying philosophical and religious teachings rather than intended for use in the context of sexual rites. Even then, such ideas represent only a minor – if colourful – strand within the history of Buddhism as a whole.

It may be helpful to explore Christian attitudes to sex further as an initial point of departure. Although attitudes have changed in modern times and Christians today have differing views, a basic feature of traditional Christian thought has been that sex should be closely linked to procreation, and that procreation is good and desirable. In the Old Testament, God expresses the desire that his creatures should 'be fruitful and multiply' (Genesis 1.22). The production of progeny is valued, and to remain unmarried was shameful in the eyes of the Old Testament. In the creation of progeny, parents were seen as playing their part in God's overall plan for creation. Although God is the ultimate author of life, through their union parents cooperate with him in the transmission of this divine gift. So important is this role that the institution that provides the social and legal framework for it, namely marriage, is given sacramental status and celebrated in church.

Buddhist reflections on sexuality have a different starting point. Buddhist teachings impose no obligation to procreate, and rather than a sign of divine bounty, Buddhist doctrine sees birth as the gateway to another round of suffering (*duḥkha*) in the cycle of *saṃsāra*. The generation of a new life is not seen in Buddhist teachings as confirmation that one is playing one's part in the unfolding of a divine plan, but on the contrary as evidence of a failure to attain nirvana. This is not to say that Buddhists see the birth of a child as an occasion for sorrow – on the contrary, it would be celebrated with joy – only that from a philosophical perspective the goal of Buddhist teachings is not to seek birth, but to put an end to it.

Yet balancing this, there is a more positive perspective from which birth can be seen as an occasion for optimism. As noted in the last chapter, to achieve what the texts call a 'precious human rebirth' is a great blessing, since according to traditional teachings rebirth as a human being provides the most favourable opportunity to attain nirvana. Furthermore, rebirth need not necessarily be seen as a futile series of repeated cycles and can be conceptualized instead as a vast ascending spiral: in this way, despite being reborn, some ground has been gained and the goal of nirvana is closer than it was before.

The dangers of sexual desire

As the Buddha's words in the text box below reveal, Buddhism in general adopts a wary attitude towards the opposite sex. This is because Buddhism is an ascetic tradition which teaches that control of the appetites and desires is a prerequisite for spiritual development. The Second Noble Truth teaches that the cause of suffering is desire or craving (*tṛṣṇā*). Erotic desires are among the strongest human beings can experience, and sex represents a potent obstacle in the quest for liberation. The Buddha said that he knew of nothing that overpowers a man's mind so much as 'the form of a woman' (A.iii.68f). Perhaps this was the reason for his oft-quoted advice to Ānanda on how monks should behave towards women.

> **Lord, how should we behave towards women?**
> **– Do not see them, Ānanda.**
>
> **But if we see them, how should we behave, Lord?**
> **– Do not speak to them, Ānanda.**
>
> **But if they speak to us, Lord, how should we behave?**
> **– Practise mindfulness, Ānanda.**
>
> **(D.ii.141)**

Such advice is, perhaps, best seen not as evidence of a misogynist streak in Buddhism (although this is often alleged) but as a realization of the danger posed by sexual desire to members of a celibate community. Monks would come into daily contact with women in the villages as they received food on their alms round, and the Buddha was well aware how easily attraction could arise. He makes similar points about female sexual desire too, warning of the dangers of the desires women feel for men. Although women are said to be 'a snare of Māra' (the Buddhist devil), it is not basically women who are the problem, nor men, but the sexual desire which the physical proximity of the genders can create and which binds both to *saṃsāra*. This mistrust of sex is not peculiar to Buddhism, and parallels can be seen in the more ascetic strands of Christianity and other religions and philosophies that teach that the way to salvation lies through the subjugation of the passions.

Marriage

For those who are unable to cope with the rigours of the celibate monastic life, the status of married householder is recommended. In Buddhism marriage is essentially a secular contract of partnership in which the partners assume obligations towards one another. Marriage is not a sacrament, and monks do not officiate at wedding ceremonies. They are also prohibited by the Vinaya from playing the role of matchmaker or go-between in bringing couples together. Nevertheless, it is customary for newlyweds to attend the local monastery later for a blessing and a simple ceremony in which texts are chanted. An early text from the Pāli canon, the *Sigālovāda Sutta*, summarizes the obligations of husband and wife as follows:

> In five ways should a wife . . . be ministered to by her husband: by respect, by courtesy, by faithfulness, by giving her authority (in the home), by providing her with adornments.

The wife reciprocates by ensuring that:

her duties are well performed, she shows hospitality to the kin of both, is faithful, watches over the goods he (her husband) brings, and shows skill and artistry in discharging all her business.

While monogamy is the preferred and predominant model, there is much local variation in marriage patterns across the Buddhist world. Early texts mention a variety of temporary and permanent arrangements entered into for both emotional and economic reasons, and in different parts of Buddhist Asia both polygamy and polyandry have been (and still are) practised. The various forms of marriage arrangements found among Buddhists are determined more by local custom than Buddhist teachings, and such matters are seen as essentially the responsibility of the secular authorities. Buddhism itself has never evolved a form of marriage ceremony and there is no 'official' Buddhist marriage service as such. Western Buddhists, however, have begun to develop marriage services modelled on the Christian one simply because church weddings are such a familiar part of everyday life in the West.

Since it does not regard marriage as a religious matter, Buddhism has no objection to divorce, but due to social pressures in traditional societies this is much less common than in the West. Some Western Buddhist groups, like the Friends of the Western Buddhist Order, have experimented with new models of community life without marriage, in order to overcome the perceived exclusiveness of the nuclear Western family unit. Some members of the group live in single-sex communities, and the Order sees an individual's sexual orientation – for example, whether straight, gay, or transgendered – as of little importance. It is felt that as one advances on the spiritual path sexuality will come to be transcended and gender stereotypes will disappear, leading to a kind of androgynous ideal state.

While lay Buddhists are free to marry and have families, there is a clear sense in Buddhism that the lay estate is inferior to the monastic one, and is appropriate only for those who are not yet able to sever the ties that bind them to the mundane world. This resembles the advice of St Paul that although a life of chastity is superior, 'it is better to marry than be aflame with passion' (1 Corinthians 7:9). Married laypeople may adopt the practice of voluntary celibacy for longer or shorter periods. For example, in South Asia it would not be uncommon for pious lay followers to abstain from sexual relations when the twice-monthly *poṣadha* ceremony is celebrated. Although there are exceptions, most notably in Japan, the Buddhist ideal has always been to abandon family life, subdue sexual desire, and live either alone or in a celibate community. In this respect, the Buddha provides the perfect role model: at the age of 29 he turned his back on family life and remained celibate for the rest of his days.

The third precept

Various precepts were laid down to regulate sexual behaviour, particularly for monks and nuns, as we will see below, while the sexual morality of the laity is governed primarily by the third precept. This precept prohibits 'misconduct (*micchācāra*) in things sexual (*kāmesu*)'. The wording of the precept is imprecise, and it does not define which forms of behaviour constitute 'misconduct'. Although it makes no explicit reference to 'coveting another man's wife', as does the Third Commandment, the third precept is almost universally interpreted in Buddhist societies to prohibit, first and foremost, adultery. Little is said about premarital sex, but the impression is given that marriage is the only appropriate forum for sexual intimacy. Some early sources specify certain classes of women who are precluded as sexual partners, such as close relatives and vulnerable young girls, and medieval commentators expand on this by including prohibited times, places, and methods of intercourse.

Other more general moral teachings also have a bearing on sexual behaviour. For example, the principle of *ahiṃsā* would require that one should not intentionally harm another person physically or emotionally, thus precluding rape, paedophilia, sexual harassment, and perhaps incest. Furthermore, all relationships, including sexual ones, should be informed by the virtues of loving-kindness (*mettā*) and compassion (*karuṇā*). The 'Golden Rule' would counsel that you should do nothing to others you would not like done to yourself. This is specifically applied to adultery at S.v.354, where it is said that just as you would not like another to commit adultery with your wife, you should not do it yourself with another man's wife. Furthermore, the *śīla* component of the Eightfold Path relating to Right Speech, Right Action, and Right Livelihood would impose certain general restraints upon conduct, such as a requirement to speak the truth and be straightforward and honest in relationships, thereby avoiding the lies and deceit common in extramarital affairs. Adultery also involves breaking the solemn vow of fidelity typically made in a wedding service, and so would be prohibited by these more general standards of moral conduct as well as by the third precept.

Ways in which the third precept can be broken, according to the commentaries

From the *Abhidharmakośa-bhāṣya* 1V.74a-b (4th century CE):

1. Intercourse with a forbidden woman, that is, the wife of another, one's mother, one's daughter, or one's paternal or maternal relations
2. Intercourse with one's own wife through a forbidden orifice
3. In an unsuitable place: an uncovered spot, a shrine or forest
4. At an unsuitable time: when the wife is pregnant, when she is nursing, or when she has taken a vow

From *The Jewel Ornament of Liberation* by sGam Po Pa (1079–1153):

1. In an improper part of the body, such as 'by way of the mouth or anus'
2. In an improper place, such as near the retinue of a guru, a monastery, a funeral monument (*stūpa*), or where many people have gathered
3. At an improper time, such as 'with a woman who has taken a vow, is pregnant or nursing a child, or in daylight'
4. Too often, for example 'more than five successive times'
5. In a generally improper way, such as by coercion, or with a man.

Homosexuality

The issue of homosexuality has provoked heated debate in many religious traditions, and has led to serious splits between liberals and traditionalists. The Anglican Church, which has almost 80 million members, convened an extraordinary meeting of church leaders in London in October 2003 in an attempt to avert a schism over the confirmation of a gay bishop in the Episcopal Church in the USA. There are signs that the same tensions are surfacing in Buddhism, although to a lesser degree.

The Buddha himself never passes judgement on the moral status of homosexual acts, and in early sources homosexuality is not discussed as a moral issue. There are, however, numerous references to homosexual practices in the context of monastic law. Any kind of sexual activity, whether of a heterosexual or homosexual nature, is prohibited by the Vinaya, and there are severe penalties for those who break the rules. Sexual intercourse is the first of the four most serious monastic offences (*pārājika-dharma*), and any monk or nun found guilty of it faces the penalty of lifelong expulsion from the community. More minor offences, such as masturbation or lewd conduct, of which many cases are reported in the Vinaya, are punished less severely.

The question of homosexuality arises specifically in connection with admission to the Order. Certain types of people were not allowed to be ordained as monks, among them hermaphrodites and a class of individuals known in the Pāli texts as *paṇḍakas*. It is not entirely clear who or what these were, but Peter Harvey concludes that the term denotes a type of 'sexually dysfunctional passive homosexual' male. Zwilling suggests that *paṇḍakas* were 'a socially stigmatised class of passive, probably transvestite, homosexuals'. These individuals were excluded from ordination by the Buddha following an incident of lewd conduct by one of their number (Vin.i.85f). At stake were both the reputation of monks and nuns with the public and the risk of disruption within the monastery which might hinder spiritual progress. However, there seems to have been no bar on the admission of non-practising homosexuals who did nothing to draw attention to their sexual orientation. Buddhism believes that gender can change from one life to another, and some Buddhists explain homosexuality as the result of a past gender reasserting itself in the present life. There are even stories in the early sources of gender changing within the same lifetime, such that due to karmic factors men become women and vice versa (Vin.iii.35), but such changes were not seen as a hindrance to spiritual progress. Sexual orientation and even gender were seen as somewhat fluid, therefore, and not in themselves morally problematic.

In modern times, however, the presence of gay monks in the Buddhist Order has become a source of controversy. In July 2003 Phra Pisarn Thammapatee, one of Thailand's most famed monks, claimed there were about a thousand gays among the country's 300,000 monks, an estimate others say is far too low. Whatever the actual number, he called for them to be expelled and for stricter screening of candidates for ordination. Expressing the view that those with 'sexual deviation' must be prevented from donning the saffron robes, he alleged that 'some homosexual monks have caused trouble in the temples'. Clearly, the presence of homosexuals in the Buddhist *sangha* in some countries is no less controversial than the presence of gay clergy in Christian denominations.

The Dalai Lama on homosexuality

In the course of the 1990s, the Dalai Lama made a number of statements on sexual ethics in his writings and in public meetings that caused concern to homosexuals in North America. Leaders of the gay and lesbian community in the San Francisco area asked for a meeting to clarify his views, and the meeting took place in San Francisco on 11 June 1997. In discussions with gay Buddhist representatives, the Dalai Lama affirmed the dignity and rights of gays and lesbians but stated that masturbation and oral or anal intercourse are improper activities and are proscribed for Buddhist practitioners. Referring to authoritative texts of the kind cited

5. The fourteenth Dalai Lama of Tibet

earlier, the Dalai Lama stated that any organ other than the vagina,
such as the mouth, anus, hands, thighs, and calves, should not be
used in sexual intercourse. He suggested that one way of looking at
these sexual proscriptions is to recognize that the purpose of
sexuality as seen in India at the time was reproduction, which
would explain why all sexual activity that cannot result in

reproduction is proscribed. However, he added that it is better for a Buddhist practitioner to engage in proscribed sexual activities if suppression of such desires would have more negative consequences, such as aggression or violence due to frustration.

The Dalai Lama pointed out that Buddhist precepts take into account the time, culture, and society in which they originate. For example, monks wore saffron because at the time it was conventional in India for poor people to wear saffron. 'If homosexuality is part of accepted norms', he suggested, 'it is possible that it would be acceptable.' 'However', he went on, 'no single person or teacher can redefine precepts. I do not have the authority to redefine these precepts since no one can make a unilateral decision or issue a decree.' He concluded, 'Such a redefinition can only come out of *sangha* discussions within the various Buddhist traditions. It is not unprecedented in the history of Buddhism to redefine issues, but it has to be done on the collective level.' He added that it would be helpful to do more research on the origins of the precepts about sex.

Are the precepts relative or absolute?

In Chapter 2, we discussed whether Buddhist ethics is relativist or absolutist, and that question has an important bearing on how the precepts are interpreted. The Dalai Lama's remarks on homosexuality betray a tension between these two positions. In terms of the first, the precept on sexual misconduct is relative to time, place, and culture and may be adapted and changed. In terms of the second, the precept expresses some universal truth about human sexuality which is immutable, namely that homosexual acts are immoral. The former offers a way out of the dilemma faced by Buddhists who are practising homosexuals by allowing the precept to be interpreted in the light of contemporary social attitudes which are more liberal than in pre-modern times. If the precept can be read against the background of the more 'enlightened' attitudes of contemporary liberal Western culture, there may be a way out of the dilemma.

However, there are problems with this strategy. The first is that if *this* provision of the third precept can be relaxed, then why not others? A parallel argument could be made for relaxing the prohibition on adultery to accommodate extramarital affairs, or allowing single people to lead a promiscuous lifestyle, on the grounds that such behaviour is no longer subject to the taboos it was in the past. The other problem is that there appears to be no suggestion that the other precepts are open to relativistic reinterpretation in the same way. No one appears to claim, for instance, that the first precept against causing harm to others, or the second precept against stealing, derive their moral authority only from ancient Indian custom and can therefore be reinterpreted as circumstances require. To make an exception in the case of the third precept for the specific purpose of legitimizing homosexual conduct, then, begins to look like special pleading.

The alternative view of the status of the precepts is to see them as defining acts which Buddhism regards as intrinsically immoral, rather than simply things that happened to be disapproved of by the society of the Buddha's day. What might be the characteristic of homosexual acts that led the Dalai Lama and other authorities to regard them as prohibited by the third precept? Clearly, the view of the high tradition, as expressed through the pens of learned commentators, is that such acts involve a perversion of the normal sexual function. As an example of decadence and moral decline, Buddhaghosa speaks of the attraction of 'men for men' and 'women for women' (DA. 853), yet this is exceptional, and homosexual attraction in itself is not generally what the texts condemn. Instead, they focus on certain *acts*, and it is important to note that the acts that are prohibited are not only prohibited for homosexuals, but also for heterosexual couples. The third precept, then, appears not to be directed against homosexuals as a group, but rather at certain forms of sexual practice. These are typically defined in the commentaries as intercourse through a 'wrong path' (*amārga*) or 'a forbidden orifice' – in other words oral or anal sex. But why should these forms of intercourse be singled out for prohibition? Unfortunately, the commentators do not explain, but one obvious common feature of these practices is that unlike normal heterosexual intercourse they cannot lead to procreation. The problem therefore appears to be not homosexuality in itself, but specific forms of sexual practice that are seen as immoral because inherently non-procreative.

Sex and procreation

Although this chapter began by drawing a contrast between Buddhist and Christian views of sexuality and reproduction, we seem to have found here a perhaps unexpected area of agreement. Ironically, although Buddhism imposes no obligation on its followers to procreate, it seems to regard as immoral sexual practices that are not open to the generation of life. But why should the procreative aspect of the sexual act be of such importance, morally speaking, from a Buddhist point of view? We can understand why Christians might think it important given the biblical emphasis on procreation, but, as already noted, Buddhism begins from a different set of premises. We can only speculate about this, but presumably the ancient authorities saw a conflict of some kind between non-reproductive sex and other important Buddhist values. Perhaps it was thought that non-reproductive sex harms the interests of beings seeking human rebirth. Heterosexual relationships provide the context for new life to come into being and for individuals to attain a 'precious human rebirth'. Heterosexual parents may therefore be thought of as cooperating in the liberation of all beings. When sexual activity is innately sterile, however (as opposed to accidentally sterile in the case of infertility, for example), the partners through their chosen form of behaviour may be seen as closing off the path to liberation which lies through a human rebirth.

But is not the same true for those who – like monks and nuns – have chosen celibacy? Do they not also turn their backs on those seeking a human rebirth? Their situation may be thought different, since their chosen form of life involves the practice of chastity. The distinction the third precept makes between acceptable and non-acceptable forms of sexual intercourse applies only to those who have chosen to live in a sexual relationship. There are further problems, however, since leaving aside those who have chosen the celibate life, the use of contraception by married couples also intentionally frustrates procreation. To be consistent in upholding traditional ethical teachings, the Dalai Lama would need to condemn the use of contraception as frustrating the procreative aspect of the sexual act since, as Perera notes, 'The orthodox Indian tradition of sex holds no brief for any form of contraception.' The Dalai Lama has stated as much himself in the *World Tibet News* (12 August 1997) saying, 'I think, basically, the purpose of sex is reproduction.' Nevertheless, he seemed to contradict this in a speech at Forum 2000 in Prague when he stated, 'I personally feel we need to be pragmatic and adopt birth control measures in order to ensure the quality of life today in developing countries, and to protect the quality of life for future generations.' It would be open to him, of course, to claim that contraception is used by many couples not to *avoid* having children but as an aid to family planning in order to ensure that they have the right number of children and at an appropriate time. Among heterosexual couples, then, even when contraception is used, the procreative dimension of their sexual relationship may not be absent in the same way it is for homosexuals.

Conclusion

Buddhist teachings on sexual ethics are by no means clearly formulated, but do appear to express the following ideals:

1) Celibacy is preferable to marriage.

2) For those who marry, the only legitimate forms of sexual conduct are those that are procreative in nature.

We also noted a close and unexpected resemblance between Tibetan Buddhist and traditional Christian teachings on sexual ethics. Certain of the Dalai Lama's pronouncements could almost have been issued by the Vatican, and his views on abortion and euthanasia also closely resemble Catholic teachings (the practice of celibacy by Buddhist and Catholic clergy is also an interesting point of similarity).

There is clearly a need, as the Dalai Lama recognizes, for further discussion on the subject of Buddhism and sexuality. Buddhism historically has had little interest in these issues, being concerned mainly to persuade people to become celibate and renounce what early texts call the 'village practice' of sexual intercourse. There is therefore much that is unclear in Buddhist teachings on sexual ethics and many points that need to be more carefully thought through. As traditional Buddhism encounters a hedonistic West where celibacy is not much in vogue, this remains an urgent area for further investigation.

Chapter 5
War and terrorism

The last century proved to be one of the bloodiest in history. War on a scale never before seen caused untold destruction and loss of life. Sadly, the present century has also begun on a belligerent note. The terrible events of 11 September 2001 in New York brought home to the world the awesome damage that can be inflicted by well-trained and coordinated terrorists who act without fear for their own lives.

In the aftermath of the attack on the World Trade Center, President Bush took the view that the battle had to be taken to the terrorists and that the safety of the world depended upon the capture and punishment of those responsible. Vowing that 'justice will be done', he played a leading part in organizing a coalition of nations that sent troops first of all to Afghanistan to fight the fundamentalist Taliban regime which was thought to be harbouring Osama bin Laden, and also in launching operation 'Iraqi Freedom' in March 2003.

Was President Bush right to respond the way he did, by choosing to fight fire with fire and following the path of aggression? Opinion around the world was divided, even in those countries whose governments supported the fight against terror. Large protest marches were organized by groups who opposed the war. Those manifesting opposition included many Buddhists and Buddhist organizations. On which Buddhist teaching was their opposition to the war based? Is Buddhism categorically opposed to war, or does it depend on the nature of the conflict? Can there be a 'just war' according to Buddhism, and what is the appropriate response for Buddhists in the face of outrages such as 9/11?

Classical sources on war

Buddhist teachings strongly oppose the use of violence, analysing it in psychological terms as the product of greed (*rāga*), hatred (*dveṣa*), and delusion (*moha*). The false belief in a self (*ātman*) and a desire to protect that self against 'others' who are thought to threaten it is seen as one underlying cause of aggression. Buddhism holds that drawing a sharp boundary between self and others leads to the construction of a self-image that sees all that is not of 'me and mine' (such as those of another country, race, or creed) as alien and threatening. When this strong sense of self is reduced by practising Buddhist teachings, such egocentric preoccupations are thought to subside and to be replaced by a greater appreciation of the kinship among beings. This dissipates the fear and hostility which engender conflict and so removes one of the main causes of violent disputes. When threatened, Buddhists are encouraged to practise patience (*kṣānti*), and there are many stories of exemplary patience as well as practices designed to cultivate toleration and forbearance. Anger is seen as a negative emotion that serves only to inflame situations and inevitably rebounds, causing negative karmic consequences.

Early Buddhist literature contains numerous references to war, and Lambert Schmithausen has reviewed the most important. The view expressed almost unanimously in the texts is that since war involves killing, and killing is a breach of the first precept, it is morally wrong to fight in either offensive or defensive wars. In marked contrast to the teachings of the Qur'an, the Buddha states (Sn iv.308–11) that warriors who die in battle go not to heaven but to a special hell, since at the moment of death their minds are intent on killing living beings. According to Schmithausen, Vasubandhu in his

Abhidharmakośabhāṣya expresses the view that a soldier, 'even if conscripted, is guilty of killing unless he makes the firm resolve that he will definitely not kill anybody, even for the sake of saving his own life'. The same text affirms that killing is bad karma even in the case of self-defence or when done for the sake of defending friends. A legend in the commentary to the *Dhammapada* narrates how the Buddha's kinsmen, the Śākyas, offered only token resistance when attacked by King Viḍūḍabha, and allowed themselves to be slaughtered rather than break the precept against taking life. The *Jātakas* contain stories concerning princes and kings who were so horrified by violence that they renounced their kingdoms to become ascetics or refused to defend themselves in the face of attack.

The example of the emperor Aśoka in the 3rd century BCE is often given as the model for a Buddhist ruler. After a bloody campaign in the 13th year of his reign, Aśoka renounced violence and vowed

From the *Dhammapada*

'He abused me, he struck me, he overpowered me, he robbed me.' Those who harbour such thoughts do not still their hatred.

(v.3)

All tremble at violence, all fear death. Comparing oneself with others one should neither kill nor cause to kill.

(v.129)

He who has renounced violence towards all living beings, weak or strong, who neither kills nor causes others to kill – him do I call a holy man.

(v.405)

henceforth to rule by Dharma. The edicts promulgated throughout his extensive empire speak of tolerance and compassion and state that conquest by Dharma is preferable to conquest by force or coercion. Aśoka modelled himself on the classical concept of the *cakravartin*, the righteous Buddhist king. It is notable, however, that although the *cakravartin* is portrayed as conquering peacefully through the power of Dharma, he nonetheless retains his army and is accompanied by it on his travels to neighbouring kingdoms. In the light of such anomalies, some scholars, such as Steven Collins and Elizabeth Harris, detect 'two modes' of Dharma in the Pāli canon with respect to violence. In the first, 'the assessement of violence is context-dependent and negotiable', and in the second it is 'context-independent and non-negotiable'. This view is based on the fact that on certain occasions the Buddha seems tacitly to accept – or at least does not explicitly condemn – the use of force by kings. A golden opportunity for him to do so occurred in the *Mahāparinibbāna Sutta* (D.ii.72ff) when the warmongering king Ajātasattu sent his chief minister to the Buddha to seek advice on his plan to attack the Vajjis. Instead of delivering a forthright condemnation of war, the Buddha simply commented on seven positive features of Vajjian society. Nevertheless, when making more explicit pronouncements on the subject, the Buddha and the classical sources as a whole unanimously favour a pacifist stance and show little sign of condoning the use of violence.

Buddhism at war

Turning from theory to practice, the pacifist ideal of the classical sources has not prevented Buddhists from fighting battles and conducting military campaigns from a mixture of political and religious motives. The historical background to the Buddhist involvement in war in different countries has been well surveyed by Peter Harvey. The early history of Sri Lanka was convulsed by war between Sinhalese and Tamils, and King Duṭṭhagāmaṇi (1st century BCE) is regarded as a national hero for defeating the Tamil general Eḷāra who had invaded the island from South India.

Dutthagāmaṇi's victory was glorified in a famous chronicle known as the *Mahāvaṃsa* (5th–6th centuries CE) which relates that his army was accompanied by Buddhist monks and that Buddhist relics adorned the spears of the soldiers. Monks disrobed and joined the army to fight in what the chronicle depicts as a 'holy war', although no such concept exists in Buddhism. Despite this apparent endorsement by the *sangha*, after his victory Dutthagāmaṇi felt remorse at the loss of life, whereupon, according to the chronicle, he was reassured by enlightened monks (*arhats*) that he was responsible for the deaths of just 'one and a half people'. The meaning of this cryptic remark seems to be that in contrast to Buddhists, Tamils count only as half persons, since they are 'evil men of wrong views' little better than 'beasts'. Later, in the 5th century, the island was threatened by three powerful South Indian kingdoms, and there were invasions by militant Hindus in the 5th, 9th, 10th, 11th and 13th centuries. In modern times, leading monks such as the late Walpola Rahula have spoken with approval of 'religio-nationalism' and described Dutthagāmaṇi's campaign as a 'crusade'. Supporters of Sinhalese nationalism include some Buddhist monks who believe that only a military defeat and the expulsion of the Tamils from the country will bring a lasting peace.

Buddhists were inevitably caught up in the turbulent history of South East Asia in the 20th century as Communist and Maoist movements fought for political power in Vietnam and Cambodia. The Khmer Rouge destroyed almost all of Cambodia's 3,600 Buddhist temples and reduced the number of monks from 50,000 to barely 3,000. The fear of Communist insurgency in Thailand led some monks to take a militant stand. In the 1970s the monk Kittivuddho made a number of controversial public statements to the effect that killing Communists in defence of the Thai nation, Buddhism, and the monarchy was a religious duty that justified the suspension of the ordinary rules of morality. He compared Communism to the devil Māra, and spoke of the destruction of Communism and the killing of Communists as an act of great merit. In a speech to soldiers he offered a utilitarian justification for his views, stating that killing 5,000 Communists in order to ensure the happiness of 42 million Thais was legitimate.

East Asia has also seen the involvement of monks in insurrections and military campaigns. This was most noticeable in Japan, where monasteries became wealthy land-owning institutions employing bands of warrior monks (*sōhei*) to provide protection and intimidate opponents. In the feudal conflicts of the medieval period, battles were fought between one sect and another and against military rulers (*shōgun*) and the imperial court. The teachings and practices of Zen Buddhism were found helpful by the military caste (*bushi*) as techniques to discipline the mind in battle and dispel the fear of death. Martial arts such as swordsmanship and archery were influenced by Zen teachings, and the doctrine of emptiness (*śūnyatā*) helped provide justification both for taking life and contemplating the loss of one's own life with equanimity. In the final analysis, so the reasoning of teachers such as Takuan Sōhō Zenji (1573–1645) went, there is only emptiness or the void: life is like a dream and the one who strikes and the one who is struck are merely phantoms.

In the modern period, Buddhist religious groups have had a close involvement with Japanese nationalism and militarism. The Zen and Pure Land denominations provided financial support for the 1937–45 war with China, and in the Second World War most

> The uplifted sword has no will of its own, it is all of emptiness. It is like a flash of lightning. The man who is about to be struck down is also of emptiness, as is the one who wields the sword [. . .] Do not get your mind stopped with the sword you raise, forget about what you are doing, and strike the enemy.
>
> Zen master Takuan Sōhō Zenji (1573–1645)

Buddhist schools (with the notable exception of Sōka Gakkai) supported the Japanese war effort against the Allies. In his recent book *Zen at War* (1998), Brian Victoria has exposed the extent to which many well-known Zen masters were enthusiastic advocates of war, to the surprise and embarrassment of many of their pacifist Western followers. The well-known Zen master Harada Daiun Sōgaku wrote, 'without plunging into the war arena, it is totally impossible to know the Buddha Dharma'. Yasutani Haku'un, well known in the West as one of the founders of the Sanbō Kyōdan school, expressed the following view on the ethics of killing in war:

> Of course one should kill, killing as many as possible. One should, fighting hard, kill everyone in the enemy army. The reason for this is that in order to carry compassion and filial obedience through to perfection it is necessary to assist good and punish evil. However, in killing one should swallow one's tears, bearing in mind the truth of killing yet not killing.

Such muddled remarks about 'killing yet not killing' are typical of the sophistry Zen masters resorted to. In his second book *Zen War Stories* (2003), Victoria cites many more examples of Buddhist militarism in Japan, and comments:

> In infusing the suicidal Japanese military spirit, especially when extended to civilians, with the power of religious belief, Japan's wartime Zen leaders revealed themselves to be *thoroughly and completely morally bankrupt*. [emphasis in original]

The leaders of Myoshin-ji, the headquarters temple of one of Japan's main Zen sects, issued a public apology for its complicity in Japanese militarism just 16 days after 9/11, giving added poignancy to the declaration.

Such militarism, however, is far from all-pervasive. In Japan, the Nipponzan Myōhōji sect supports pacifism and opposes nuclear weapons. Monks from the group can often be seen on peace protests chanting and beating their drums. The Nipponzan Myōhōji has also

6. Ven. Nichidatsu Fujii, founder of the Nipponzan Myōhōji

built over sixty 'Peace Pagodas' in Japan, as well as five in India and
two each in Sri Lanka, the UK, and the USA. The group hopes that
the pagodas and the sacred relics they house will exert a calming
influence on a troubled world. Elsewhere in Japan, Daisetsu Ikeda,
president of Sōka Gakkai International (SGI), has been an active
peace campaigner for many years. The objectives of SGI include the
aim of 'Working for peace by opposing all forms of violence and
contributing to the welfare of humankind by pursuing humanistic
culture and education.' Another group active on this front is the
Rissho Kosei-kai, which in 1978 established the Niwano Peace
Foundation 'to contribute to the realization of world peace.'

In the aftermath of the Chinese invasion of Tibet in 1959, it is estimated that 6 million Tibetans died and a further million fled the country as refugees. Despite a systematic and brutal programme to suppress Buddhism, the Dalai Lama, the *de facto* leader of Tibet's Buddhists, has consistently adopted a policy of non-violent resistance, in recognition of which he was awarded the Nobel Peace Prize in 1989.

Compartmentalization of values

From the foregoing, it seems that with respect to war there is a tension in Buddhism between precept and practice. Killing is wrong, but nevertheless wars are fought for and not uncommonly justified by religious reasons. Schmithausen describes this as a 'compartmentalization of values' which in extreme cases is 'almost schizoid'. In South Asia the tension between saying one thing and doing another was eased to some degree by subsequent merit-producing activities such as making lavish donations to the Order, whereas in Japan and parts of East Asia the dissonance generally seems not to have troubled people to such a great extent.

The facts set out above problematize the issue of war and peace from a Buddhist perspective. The usual image of Buddhism as a peace-loving religion that recoils in horror from violence and whose followers shrink from even treading on an ant is clearly incomplete. Furthermore, while many Buddhists would identify themselves as pacifists, this moral stance embraces a range of possible positions. For example, does being a pacifist mean that one is opposed to:

a) war;
b) the taking of life in any form (for example, as was Albert Schweitzer);
c) all violence (as were Gandhi and Martin Luther King);
d) the use of force by private citizens but not by the state (as was St Augustine); or
e) any use of physical force at all?

It is clearly important to explore the basis of Buddhist pacifism and discover what precisely is being opposed. For example, while most civilized people are instinctively opposed to 'violence', a distinction can be made between violence and force. While violence connotes aggression, force need not, and we must be careful not to prejudice the discussion by conflating the two terms. Force is morally neutral: it takes force to turn a prayer wheel or carry survivors to safety in the aftermath of a terrorist attack. The position in e) above that 'any use of physical force is wrong' therefore seems simplistic and to exclude too much. To make a judgement, we need to know something of the particular circumstances in which force is to be used and also to evolve criteria that will tell us which uses of force are justified and which not.

At this point, some difficult questions present themselves. If any use of force is ruled out, as the early texts suggest, how will it be possible to restrain deranged individuals who might harm themselves and others, or violent criminals who threaten innocent citizens? If complete pacifism is required by Buddhism, it seems hard to imagine how a criminal justice system can function. The police would be unable to carry out their duties, prisons would be unworkable institutions, and anarchy would be the likely outcome. Since no Buddhist country has abolished the rule of law or is without some means to enforce it (such as an army or police force), it seems that Buddhist moral principles must allow for some use of force if a stable society – itself a Buddhist ideal – is to be achieved. And if the use of force is justified *within* the borders of a state, might it not on occasion be justified outside, in a military campaign?

The concept of a 'just war'

There is little guidance from Buddhist thinkers on questions of the kind raised above. The assumption seems to have been that such matters were for the political authorities to deal with and were not appropriate subjects for religious concern. There are passing references to war in some commentaries, but there is no explicit and systematic body of philosophical literature explaining how one accommodates the pacifist ideal to the realities of social and political life. What is needed to begin to address these questions is a set of 'bridging principles' which through the use of practical reason will allow conclusions to be drawn as to how values such as *ahiṃsā* should direct conduct in concrete situations.

In the West, such a set of principles is found in a body of theory concerned with the notion of the 'just war'. One of the earliest thinkers to ponder this question was St Augustine (354–430 CE) and his ideas were greatly developed and refined by St Thomas Aquinas (1224–1274). Thereafter many jurists and philosophers, such as Francisco de Vitoria (1548–1617), Francisco Suarez (1548–1617), Hugo Grotius (1583–1645), Samuel Pufendorf (1632–1704), Christian Wolff (1679–1754), and Emerich de Vattel (1714–1767), made a contribution. Christian thinkers developed the doctrine because of a perceived conflict between, on the one hand, the need to defend Christian communities and states against attack and, on the other, religious teachings such as the commandment against killing and the injunction to 'turn the other cheek' (Matt 5.38–41). In modern times, interest in the concept of a just war has been revived as moralists, politicians, and military strategists ponder the moral dilemmas arising from the invention of nuclear weapons, the need to intervene in situations such as Kosovo, and most recently the 'war on terror'.

Just war thinking has two main branches. The first concerns the conditions that need to be satisfied for going to war and is summed up in the Latin phrase *jus ad bellum* ('rightness in going to war'). The second, known as *jus in bello* ('rightness in the conduct of war'), concerns things it is legitimate and not legitimate to do once a military campaign has been initiated. The general consensus among theorists is that five conditions need to be satisfied for war to be declared, and once battle has been joined two broad principles govern its conduct. The five conditions may be stated in various ways, but a typical formulation is set out in the text box overleaf.

Principles of the just war

A. *Jus ad bellum*

1. A war is just only if it is waged by a legitimate authority. Even just causes cannot be served by individuals or groups who do not constitute a legitimate authority.
2. A just war can only be fought to redress a wrong suffered. For example, self-defence against an armed attack is always considered to be a just cause (although the justice of the cause is not in itself sufficient – see point 4). Further, a just war can only be fought with 'right' intentions: the only permissible objective of a just war is to redress the injury.
3. A just war can only be waged as a last resort. All non-violent options must be exhausted before the use of force can be justified.
4. A war can only be just if it is fought with a reasonable chance of success. Deaths and injury incurred in a hopeless cause are not morally justifiable.
5. The ulimate goal of a just war is to re-establish peace. More specifically, the peace established after the war must be preferable to the peace that would have prevailed if the war had not been fought.

B. *Jus in bello*

1. The violence used in the war must be *proportional* to the injury suffered.
2. The weapons used in war must *discriminate* between combatants and non-combatants. Civilians are never permissible targets of war, and every effort must be taken to avoid killing civilians.

The just war tradition of reflection gives some general guidance on when it is morally right to go to war and against whom it is justifiable to wage war. However, it evolved at a time when the outcome of a war often depended on a single pitched battle, and applying its provisions to the infinitely more complex situations of modern warfare is not always easy. Furthermore, when the enemy mingles with civilians and cannot easily be identified, as in the case of terrorist groups, we seem to face new situations never envisaged by traditional thinkers. Nevertheless, just war theory may provide a starting point for reflection on the circumstances in which force may be legitimately used by Buddhist rulers.

Terrorism

'Terrorism' is not an easy term to define since, as commonly noted, once man's terrorist is another man's freedom fighter. Groups who are characterized as 'terrorist' today can tomorrow constitute the official government of a country, as in the case of the African National Congress, which was designated as a terrorist organization by Britain and the United States in 1987 but subsequently came to form the government of South Africa. The term 'terrorist' was originally coined and applied in self-reference by French revolutionaries in the 1790s, but few people today would welcome the epithet 'terrorist', preferring to describe themselves as 'freedom fighters', 'urban guerillas', or even 'holy warriors'.

The Wordnet online dictionary at Princeton University defines terrorism as 'the calculated use of violence (or threat of violence) against civilians in order to attain goals that are political or religious or ideological in nature; this is done through intimidation or coercion or instilling fear'. This definition makes clear why terrorism is regarded as immoral in terms of just war theory: terrorist groups do not constitute a legitimate political authority (condition 1 of the *jus ad bellum* provisions) and they specifically target civilians in their attacks in order to spread terror among the population at large (contrary to condition 2 of the *jus in bello* requirements).

Since the attack on the World Trade Center in New York, the al-Qaeda terrorist organization has been linked to bombings in Tunisia, Pakistan, Yemen, Kuwait, Bali, Moscow, Mombasa, and Madrid. What is the appropriate Buddhist response in the face of terrorist attacks of this kind? Is it legitimate to declare a 'war on terror', or is there a better way to deal with problems of international security?

Buddhist responses to terrorism have tended to make three main points. First, that we must try to understand fully the causes that have led to the present situation. The doctrine of dependent origination (*pratītya-samutpāda*) teaches that all situations are the product of a complex nexus of causes and conditions, and lasting solutions cannot be found until we fully understand the reasons why situations arise. Second, that we must respond to aggression with compassion as opposed to hatred; and third, that violence will only lead to a cycle of retaliation and make the chances of peace even more remote. The need for reflection and self-criticism was also mentioned by some, including Thich Nhat Hanh. After the attacks on 11 September 2001, he expressed the view that America would have been better off with dialogue. Identifying the key question as 'Why would anyone hate us enough to do that?',

A Buddhist on terrorism

Aung San Suu Kyi is the leader of the Burmese democracy movement and winner of the 1991 Nobel Peace Prize:

You know, I am a Buddhist. As a Buddhist, the answer is very simple and clear. That is compassion and mercy is the real panacea. I am sure that, when we have compassion and mercy in our heart, we can overcome not only terrorism but also many other evil things that are plaguing the world.

he offered the response 'If we are able to listen, they will tell us.'

Conclusion

It seems that when confronting the issues of war and terrorism, Buddhists are pulled in two different directions. On the one hand, the classical sources teach strict pacifism, while on the other Buddhist states have not been averse to the use of force, and have frequently invoked religion as a justification for military campaigns (it should be noted that war has rarely – if ever – been used by Buddhists for purposes of religious coercion). While pacifism may be a viable option for those who have renounced the world, it is not clear that it can provide a workable basis for a society. The prohibition on the use of force even in self-defence also runs counter to the moral intuition of many people. Of course, any reasonable person would do well to pay heed to the three points made again and again by Buddhists, namely the importance of seeking to understand the causes of a conflict, showing compassion to opponents, and endeavouring to resolve disputes by peaceful means. It has been wisely said that 'pacifism does not mean passivism', and there is much useful work that can be done to remove injustice and the causes of dissent before they erupt into violent conflict.

Chapter 6
Abortion

How do Buddhist ethical teachings like *ahiṃsā* affect its approach to abortion? Is Buddhism 'pro-life' or 'pro-choice'? The Buddhist belief in rebirth clearly introduces a new dimension to the abortion debate. For one thing, it puts the question 'When does life begin?' – a key question in the context of abortion – in an entirely new light. For Buddhism, life is a continuum with no discernible starting point, and birth and death are like a revolving door through which an individual passes again and again.

But does belief in rebirth increase or reduce the seriousness of abortion? It may be thought that it reduces it, since all that has been done is to postpone rebirth to a later time – the child that was to have been born simply arrives later. Traditional sources, however, do not take this view, and regard the intentional killing of a human being at any stage of life as wrong, regardless of the fact that he or she will be born again.

Buddhist embryology

The Buddha divided the stages of childbearing into four: the fertile period, pregnancy, birth, and nursing (M.ii.148). In keeping with traditional Indian medical thought, he explained conception as a natural process that occurs when three specific conditions are fulfilled (M.i.256). On this understanding, i) intercourse must take place ii) during the woman's fertile period, and iii) there must be available the spirit (*gandharva*) of a deceased person seeking rebirth. Early Buddhists shared the beliefs of the ancient Indian medical tradition known as Āyurveda regarding the reproductive process. On this understanding, pustules of blood collect in the womb and in the normal menstrual cycle break and flow forth, causing a monthly period. When the period ceases, a residue of blood remains and the womb is fertile for a period of between three to ten days. When intercourse takes place, the semen mingles with menstrual blood, and if a *gandharva* is available it 'descends' into the union of semen and blood – this is 'conception'. The gender of the individual was thought to be determined at this time (although in exceptional cases it could change during life, as we have seen) and from conception onwards the spiritual and material components that constitute the new individual – what Buddhists call *nāma-rūpa* (mind and body) – evolve together and remain united 'like a mixture of milk and water' until they once again separate at death.

Once consciousness has 'descended' into the womb and conception has occurred, the embryo develops through a set number of stages. In *The Path of Purification* (236), Buddhaghosa lists four stages of the early embryo during the first month after conception. The first stage is the *kalala*, in which the tiny embryo is described as 'clear and translucent', and is likened to 'a drop of purest oil on the tip of a hair'. The following three stages are the *abudda*, the *pesi*, and the *ghana*, terms that connote increasing density and solidity. The stages of embryonic development are summarized in an 18th-century Tibetan treatise entitled *The lamp thoroughly illuminating the presentation of the three basic bodies*. This confirms that the early views remained influential and underwent little modification. It relates how following intercourse the 'drops of semen and blood . . . are mixed in the mother's womb', and the consciousness of the intermediate being enters into this mixture. 'Initially', we are informed, 'the oval-shaped fetus is covered on the outside by something like the cream on top of boiled milk; but inside it is very runny.' It was thought that, 'The place in the semen and blood where the consciousness initially enters becomes the heart', and that in this initial phase of development 'the top and bottom [of the body at this point] are thin, and the middle is bulbous like the shape of a fish'. The text goes on to describe the course of development within the next 28 days:

> When the oval-shaped foetus has passed seven days . . . [it] becomes viscous both outside and inside, like yogurt, but has not become flesh. When another seven days pass . . . the foetus becomes fleshy but cannot withstand pressure. After another seven days it hardens . . . [so that] the flesh is now hard and can bear pressure. When this, in turn, has passed seven days . . . the foetus develops legs and arms, in the sense that five protuberances – signs of the two thighs, two shoulders and head – stand out clearly.

The sources cited by this text are in broad agreement that the length of a normal pregnancy is 38 weeks: one source places it at 268 days and another at 270 days.

Abortion and the precepts

Interpreting the traditional teachings in the light of modern scientific discoveries such as ovulation, the most common view among Buddhists today, particularly those from traditional countries, is that fertilization is the point at which individual human life commences. As a consequence, abortion is widely seen as contrary to the first precept. As already noted, the precept prohibits causing harm to anything which has *pāṇa* (Skt. *prāṇa*), which means both 'life' and 'breath'. Because of the reference to 'breath' here, it could be argued that since a fetus does not breathe, it does not fall within the scope of the precept. The sense of the term *pāṇa*, however, is not restricted to respiration and rather connotes the idea of 'vital breath' or the 'breath of life'. In medical contexts *pāṇa* is one of the bodily humours, understood as the force underlying biological growth, perhaps equivalent to the contemporary notion of metabolism. Since this process occurs throughout all stages of fetal life, it is difficult to argue that the moral protection of the first precept does not apply to the unborn. Moreover, since this metabolic process continues throughout gestation (and beyond), it is difficult to ground arguments that seek to draw a line at a certain stage of fetal development – such as viability, which occurs around the 24th week – in order to establish a point up to which abortion may be allowed.

Any ambiguity there may be thought to be in the first precept with respect to abortion is removed in the equivalent precept in the Vinaya (the third *pārājika*) which prohibits taking a human life (*manussa-viggaha*). One formulation of the precept (see text box below) explicitly mentions abortion, and the commentary explains that the prohibition applies from the moment of conception. Although strictly speaking this precept applies only to monks and nuns, it confirms that life was thought to begin at conception rather than some later point.

Despite the condemnation of abortion, the case histories recorded in the Vinaya disclose that as medical practitioners monks

---

The third *pārājika*, the monastic precept against taking human life

An ordained monk should not intentionally deprive a living thing of life even if it is only an ant. A monk who deliberately deprives a human being of life, even to the extent of causing an abortion, is no longer a follower of the Buddha. As a flat stone broken asunder cannot be put back together again, a monk who deliberately deprives a human being of life is no longer a follower of the Buddha.

(Vin.i.97)

---

occasionally became illegally involved in procuring and performing abortions. Monks frequently acted as counsellors to families, and often were drawn into the kinds of problems that arise in family life, such as an unwanted pregnancy. The motives reported in the sources for seeking an abortion include concealing extramarital affairs, as when a married woman becomes pregnant by her lover, seeking to prevent an inheritance by aborting the rightful heir prior to birth, and domestic rivalry between co-wives due to the pregnancy of one affecting the position and status of another. Sometimes monks brought their medical knowledge to bear in an attempt to cause a miscarriage. The methods used included ointments, potions, and charms, pressing or crushing the womb, and scorching or heating it. Monks who were involved in performing or procuring abortions were expelled from the *sangha* for life, the severest sanction available.

Other more popular literature describes the evil karmic consequences of abortion, sometimes in lurid detail. Stories in the *Dhammapada* commentary, the *Petavatthu* (Stories of the Departed), and the *Jātakas* (such as the *Saṃkicca Jātaka*) narrate the evil consequences which follow an abortion, such as the loss of offspring in future lives, acts of revenge, and rebirth in hell. At both a popular and scholarly level, therefore, the early teachings are consistent in depicting abortion as an immoral act that brings karmic suffering in its wake.

Human beings and persons

Much of the philosophical discussion of abortion in the West has focused on the criteria of moral personhood and the point at which a fetus acquires the capacities that entitle it to moral respect. The philosophical foundations for this approach were laid by Locke and Kant, who argued that only rational beings are 'persons' with moral status. For them, the paradigm moral subject is the adult in possession of all his or her intellectual faculties. Locke and Kant did not apply these conclusions to abortion, but building on their views contemporary philosophers who take a liberal position on abortion argue that what we value about human beings is not life *per se*, in the biological sense, but rather the various faculties and powers human beings possess, such as reason, self-consciousness, autonomy, the capacity to form relationships, and similar abilities of this kind. When these faculties are present, they say, we can speak of a moral 'person', and when they are absent there is only biological life. On this reasoning, before it acquires these attributes a fetus is only a 'potential person' rather than an actual one, and so does not have a claim to full moral status and the right to life that entails.

As an example of this approach, contemporary feminist writers such as Mary Anne Warren have identified five features central to personhood – consciousness, reasoning, self-motivated activity, the capacity to communicate, and self-awareness. Warren claims that a fetus is no more conscious or rational than a fish, and that accordingly abortion is not immoral. Opponents have responded by pointing to the vagueness and arbitrariness of the criteria suggested (for instance, are the movements of a fetus in the womb, such as kicking, a form of 'communication' with its mother?) and the difficulty of determining when and to what degree faculties such as reasoning are present. Conservative opponents use 'slippery-slope' arguments against the liberal position, claiming that a secure line cannot be drawn at any one point in the development of the fetus. They suggest that such lines are vague and can usually be pushed back down the slope of fetal development towards conception as the only clear point of origin for individual human life.

Persons and *skandhas*

A Buddhist pro-choice argument paralleling that based on the concept of personhood could be mounted by reference to the doctrine of the five aggregates (*skandhas*). These are the five factors that constitute the individual human being, as shown in the text box overleaf.

> ### The five aggregates (*skandhas*) that make up the nature of the human being
>
> 1. material form (*rūpa*)
> 2. feelings and sensations (*vedanā*)
> 3. perceptions (*saṃjñā*)
> 4. volitions (*saṃskāra*)
> 5. consciousness (*vijñāna*)

If it could be shown, for instance, that these five endowments were acquired gradually rather than all at once, it may be possible to argue that the life of an early fetus which possessed fewer of the five was less valuable than that of a more mature one, which possessed them all. The second aggregate relating to the faculty of feeling, for instance, may be thought of as absent or not well developed in an embryo or very young fetus, since the capacity to feel depends on the development of a brain and central nervous system. This argument faces the problem that according to the early commentarial tradition all five *skandhas* are present from the moment of rebirth (in other words, from conception). Buddhaghosa, for instance, is very clear in stating that the human mind-body aggregate (*nāma-rūpa*) is complete in the very first moment of existence as a human being. This means that the body (*rūpa*) and the other four aggregates of feelings (*vedanā*), conceptions (*saṃjñā*), mental formations (*saṃskāra*), and consciousness (*vijñāna*) form a unity from the outset rather than developing gradually as the fetus evolves.

The doctrine of rebirth, moreover, sees the new conceptus as not just a 'potential person' evolving for the first time from nothing, but as a continuing entity bearing the complete karmic encoding of a recently deceased individual. If we rewind the karmic tape a short way, perhaps just a few hours, to the point when death occurred in the previous life, we would typically find an adult man or woman fulfilling all the requirements of 'personhood'. The bodily form at rebirth has changed, but the bodily form of human beings changes constantly, and according to Buddhist teachings we have before us at conception the same individual only now at an immature state of physical development. Given the continuity of the human subject through thousands of lifetimes, it seems arbitrary to apply labels such as 'actual' or 'potential' to any given stage and to claim that the individual repeatedly gains and then loses the moral protection of the first precept.

It is sometimes suggested that Buddhism regards late abortions as morally worse than earlier ones. This view is based on a remark of Buddhaghosa in his commentary on the Vinaya (MA.i.198) to the effect that the size of the victim is one of two important criteria (the other being sanctity) in assessing the gravity of breaches of the first precept. Since a fetus is considerably larger at the end of its term, it has been argued that late abortions are worse than earlier ones. This line of argument, however, fails to appreciate that Buddhaghosa's comments with respect to size were made purely with reference to animals. Thus, as we saw in Chapter 3, it is worse to kill a large animal, such as an elephant, than a mouse, because it involves a greater degree of effort and determination, and the will to cause harm on the part of the assailant is greater. Clearly, the criterion of size is not meant to be applied in the case of human beings, otherwise it would lead to the ludicrous conclusion that killing large people was worse than killing small people. The argument that early abortions are morally less serious because the fetus is smaller, therefore, is based upon a misunderstanding of Buddhaghosa's criterion.

Abortion in Buddhist countries

Turning now to the contemporary situation, things are much less tidy and consistent than they appear in the classical sources. There is considerable variation across the Buddhist world, much divergence between theory and practice, and a fair amount of what might be called 'moral dissonance', whereby individuals experience themselves as pulled in contradictory directions.

Thailand

Given the attitude to abortion in the classical scriptures, in the more traditional Buddhist countries such as Sri Lanka and Thailand, abortion is illegal with certain limited exceptions, such as when necessary to save the mother's life or in the case of rape. The relevant Thai law is the Penal Code of 1956, which imposes strict penalties: a woman who causes an abortion for herself or procures one from someone else can expect to face a penalty of three years in prison and a fine of 3,000 baht, or both. The penalty for the abortionist is even greater: five years or 5,000 baht, or both, and if the woman is injured or killed in the process the penalties are much more severe. Official statistics from the 1960s report some five abortions per year, but this massively underestimates the number of abortions performed. This is because illegal abortions are very common, with perhaps 300,000 such procedures a year in Thailand performed in the many hundreds of illegal abortion clinics, found throughout the country but particularly in rural areas. This figure is equivalent to 37 abortions per 1,000 women of childbearing age. By way of comparison, some statistics from other countries are: Canada, 11.1; USA, 24.2; Hungary, 35.3; Japan, 22.6 (officially, but probably between 65 and 90); Singapore, 44.5; in the former USSR the figure was an astonishing 181. According to a 1987 study, the majority of abortions (around 80–90%) in Thailand were performed for married woman, mostly agricultural workers. The study also confirmed that abortion was the accepted method of birth control among these women, suggesting that if better contraception was available the number of abortions would drop sharply.

Despite the basic religious objection to abortion, Thai attitudes towards the issue are complex and researchers often encounter contradictory positions. A 1998 survey mainly of medical staff in Thailand revealed ambivalent attitudes, with most respondents reporting negative feelings after the procedure, including 36% who were concerned about the bad karma likely to result from it. While nearly all medical staff supported abortions for women who had been raped, who were HIV positive, or who had contracted German measles in the first trimester of pregnancy, 70% were opposed to abortion on socio-economic grounds. Similarly, while a very high proportion of those surveyed viewed abortion as a threat to Thai values, 55% of the medical staff favoured a liberalization of Thai abortion laws.

One interesting aspect of the Thai situation is the low profile maintained by Buddhist monks, who rarely comment or become involved on one side or the other of the argument. With rare exceptions, monks do not picket abortion clinics, go on protest marches, or counsel women who are considering having an abortion, as clergy or activists in the West might do. This is not because they have no position on the matter, and if pressed almost all would agree that abortion is immoral. For the most part, however, they prefer to regard it as a secular or 'village' matter in which they have no direct involvement, and seem content to leave the decision to the conscience of the individuals involved. To a large extent this apparent aloofness has to do with matters of decorum and the high status in which the monkhood is held. Most Buddhist layfolk, and particularly women, would feel embarrassment at discussing such intimate matters with monks, and prefer to discuss the problem with a doctor or other secular professional. Many monks, too, feel that these questions are not proper for one who has renounced the world and is pursuing the spiritual life. This attitude is changing, although slowly.

Japan

Elsewhere in Asia, attitudes and practices relating to abortion vary quite widely. In Japan (where Buddhism has been influential but is not the state religion), abortion is legal and around a million abortions are performed each year. This compares with a figure of 1.3 million for the United States, a country with over twice the population of Japan (the annual total for the United Kingdom is around 180,000).

What many see as a constructive contribution to the dilemma posed by abortion has been developed in recent decades by Japanese Buddhists. The issue of abortion has been particularly acute in Japan because the contraceptive pill has not been widely available, apparently because of concerns about possible side effects. In the absence of effective prevention, an efficient (and profitable) abortion industry has emerged to deal with the problem of unwanted pregnancies. Faced with the anguish these situations create, Japanese society has searched its ancient cultural heritage and evolved a unique solution, in the form of the *mizuko kuyō*

7. Jizō Bosatsu

memorial service for aborted children. Only ever resorted to by a minority of women who had abortions or miscarriages, the ritual became extremely popular in the 1960s and 1970s, although it is now less common.

'*Mizuko*' literally means 'water child', a concept that has its origins in Japanese mythology, and '*kuyō*' means a ritual or ceremony. The *mizuko kuyō* service is generally a simple one in which a small figure of the bodhisattva Jizō represents the departed child. Jizō Bosatsu is a popular bodhisattva in Japan who is regarded as the protector of young children, and statues and shrines to him are found throughout the country. He is often shown dressed in the robes of a monk carrying a staff with six rings on it, which jingle like a child's rattle. The rings represent the six realms of rebirth in traditional Buddhist teachings, and Jizō visits each of these realms to help those in need. Jizō's origins lie in India as the bodhisattva Kṣitigarbha ('womb of the earth'), but when his cult reached Japan he became associated with a folk-belief concerning the fate of children who die young, known as *mizuko* or 'water babies'. Such children were thought to go to an underworld or realm of the shades, a limbo in which they awaited rebirth. In the popular imagination, this place was identified with a deserted river-bank called Sai-no-kawara in Meido. There, they seek to amuse themselves by day playing with pebbles on the beach, but when night comes they become cold and afraid, and it is then that Jizō comes to enfold them in his robe and cheer them with the jingling sound of his staff. This scene is often depicted in statues and described in hymns such as the one shown in the text box overleaf which is often recited in the course of the *mizuko kuyō* ritual.

Often a small image of Jizō (known as a *mizuko Jizō*) is decorated with a child's bib, and pinwheels and toys are placed alongside. Traditionally, the image would be placed in the home or at a small roadside shrine, but in recent years specialist temples such as the Hasedera temple in Kamakura have appeared which offer commemorative services of various degrees of sophistication. These

A hymn to Jizō often used in the *mizuko kuyō* liturgy

Be not afraid, little dear ones,
You were so little to come here,
All the long journey to Meido!

I will be Father and Mother,
Father and Mother and Playmate,
To all the children in Meido!

Then he caresses them kindly,
Folding his shining robes around them,
Lifting the smallest and frailest
Into his bosom, and holding
His staff for the stumblers to clutch.

To his long sleeves cling the infants,
Smile in response to his smiling,
Glad in his beauteous compassion.

temples are like memorial parks or cemeteries, with rows and rows of small statues each commemorating a terminated pregnancy or miscarriage. The *mizuko kuyō* ceremony can take many forms, but would typically involve the parents, and sometimes other members of the family, erecting an image of Jizō and paying their respects to it by bowing, lighting a candle, striking gongs, chanting verses or a hymn, and perhaps reciting a short Buddhist *sūtra* such as the *Heart Sūtra*. It is also customary to provide a memorial tablet and a posthumous Buddhist name, which allows the deceased child to be recognized within the family structure. The rite may be repeated at intervals, such as on the anniversary of the abortion.

8. Mizuko Jizō memorial at Raikoji (Kamakura, Japan)

The public nature of the ceremonial simultaneously acknowledges the child that has been lost and helps those involved come to terms with the event on an emotional level. Women who have the ritual performed find it consoling, and it is clearly comforting to think that Jizō is protecting their lost offspring.

One American Zen Buddhist group, the Diamond Sangha, has produced a liturgy that can be performed following an abortion or

> The blessing of the child I had expected
> Vanished like a dream.
> How bitter not to be able to cuddle my child.
> As I secretly visit the *mizuko* resting place
> I offer this lotus flower from the last *kuyō*.
> May it be a penitential proof of my love.
>
> Verse from a popular song about the
> *mizuko kuyō* ceremony

miscarriage modelled on the Japanese practice. Some non-Buddhist Western clergy have also shown interest in following the Japanese example by developing a Christian version of the *mizuko kuyō* ritual for use in churches in the West. The ritual, however, is not without its critics. The majority of Buddhist organizations in Japan do not endorse *mizuko kuyō*, regarding it as a modern innovation based on questionable theology and lacking any basis in the *sūtras*. One of the largest Buddhist organizations in Japan, the Jōdō Shinshū, actively opposes the rite for this reason, pointing out that according to orthodox Buddhist teachings a ritual cannot wipe away the bad karma caused by an abortion. The more unscrupulous temples in Japan have also sometimes exploited the ritual commercially, promoting the idea of *tatari*, or retribution from departed spirits. The idea has been put about, often accompanied by lurid pictures, that an aborted fetus becomes a vengeful spirit that causes problems for the mother unless placated by the ritual. Undoubtedly, many temples saw the ritual simply as a money-making scheme and ruthlessly exploited vulnerable women.

Opposition on the part of the Jōdō Shinshū and others, however, has not taken a political form, and Japanese Buddhists have not campaigned to change the law on abortion or sought to influence the practice of the medical profession. Japan has not seen the kinds of attacks on abortion clinics and their personnel that have taken place in the USA. This approach is in line with the non-judgemental stance Buddhism traditionally adopts on moral issues. It recognizes that the pressures and complexities of daily life can cloud the judgement and lead people to make wrong choices. The appropriate response in these cases, however, is thought to be compassion and understanding rather than vociferous condemnation.

Conclusion

Early scriptural sources oppose abortion, regarding it as a breach of the first precept, a view generally followed in traditional countries despite the evidence that large numbers of 'back-street' abortions are carried out. Some contemporary Buddhists, especially in the West, however, feel that there is more to be said on the morality of abortion than is found in the ancient sources, and that there may be circumstances in which abortion may be justified. For one thing, early Buddhist attitudes were formulated in a society that took a very different view of the status of women from that of the modern West. Feminist writers have drawn attention to the patriarchal nature of traditional societies and to the institutionalized repression of women down the centuries (other scholars deny that either of these historical claims is correct, except at specific times and places). It has also been argued that abortion rights are integral to the emancipation of women and are necessary to redress injustice. Buddhists who are sympathetic to this view and who support the notion of the woman's 'right to choose' may recommend meditation and discussion with a Buddhist teacher as ways in which the woman can get in touch with her feelings and come to a decision in harmony with her conscience. As the encounter between Buddhism and Western values proceeds, discussions over the abortion question are certain to continue, hopefully producing more light and less heat than has been the tendency in the past.

Chapter 7
Suicide and euthanasia

On 11 June 1963, the 73-year-old Vietnamese monk Thich Quang Duc burned himself alive on a main street in Saigon, making headlines around the world. Sitting calmly in the lotus posture, the elderly monk ordered two of his followers to douse him with petrol and then calmly set himself alight. The American journalist David Halberstam witnessed the dramatic scene:

> Flames were coming from a human being; his body was slowly withering and shriveling up, his head blackening and charring. In the air was the smell of burning flesh . . . Behind me I could hear the sobbing of the Vietnamese who were now gathering. I was too shocked to cry, too confused to take notes or ask questions, too bewildered to even think.

In contrast to the shock and distress of those around him, the venerable monk remained still and serene. The well-known photograph reproduced here of him sitting calmly while his body burned in the flames became one of the defining images of the 1960s.

Thich Quang Duc's suicide was a protest against the religious policies of the dictator Ngo Dinh Diem, who had persistently favoured the country's Catholic minority. Thich Quang Duc's final testimony read:

9. The suicide of Buddhist monk Thich Quang Duc in Saigon, 1963

> Before closing my eyes to go to Buddha, I have the honour to present my words to President Diem, asking him to be kind and tolerant towards his people and enforce a policy of religious equality.

Apart from the political statement it made, this dramatic image brought Buddhism to the attention of many in the West, and awakened curiosity about a religion whose followers were capable of acting with such conviction while manifesting a deep sense of inner peace and serenity and possessing apparently superhuman self-control.

What was the significance of this act, and how should it be assessed from an ethical perspective? Was Thich Quang Duc a fanatic or a martyr? Was his heroic self-sacrifice in accordance with Buddhist teachings, or was he an extremist bent on seeking publicity? Buddhist leaders in Vietnam sanctioned his suicide, and also that of another elderly monk, Thich Tieu Dieu, but apparently refused

> The press spoke then of suicide, but in the essence, it is not.
> It is not even a protest. What the monks said in the letters
> they left before burning themselves aimed only at alarming,
> at moving the hearts of the oppressors, and at calling the
> attention of the world to the suffering endured then by
> the Vietnamese. To burn oneself by fire is to prove that
> what one is saying is of the utmost importance . . . . The
> Vietnamese monk, by burning himself, says with all his
> strength and determination that he can endure the greatest
> of sufferings to protect his people . . . . To express will by
> burning oneself, therefore, is not to commit an act of
> destruction but to perform an act of construction, that is, to
> suffer and to die for the sake of one's people. This is not
> suicide.
>
> Thich Nhat Hanh, *Vietnam: Lotus in a Sea of Fire*

permission for younger monks to do likewise. Three years later, in
1966, the militant wing of the Unified Buddhist Church was
involved in another self-immolation, that of the nun Thich Nu
Thanh Quang, aged 55, although official statements indicated she
had not received permission. The militant leader Thich Tri Quang
declared, 'Burning oneself to death is the noblest form of struggle
which symbolizes the spirit of nonviolence of Buddhism.' In the
aftermath of this statement, five deaths occurred, at which point Tri
Quang called on his followers to desist. In recent decades the policy
of the Church has apparently been to dissuade its followers from
killing themselves.

Not all Buddhists were as enthusiastic about these suicides as Thich
Tri Quang. While some interpreted them as heroic acts of self-
sacrifice in accordance with the bodhisattva ideal, others saw them
as misguided and contrary to Buddhist teachings. They seemed to

some to involve both violence and the squandering of a 'precious human rebirth'.

The disagreements over the Vietnamese suicides illustrate the problematic nature of suicide as a moral issue. One problem in making a moral judgement in such cases is that we can never be completely sure of the motives of the person concerned, since he or she cannot be called to give evidence. Another complication is that it is not always easy to define what counts as 'suicide'. If we take as our definition of suicide something like 'cases where a person knowingly embarks on a course of action that will lead to his death', we may find that the category is too broad. For instance, is the soldier who throws himself on a grenade to save his comrades 'commiting suicide'? And what of the martyr who refuses to recant knowing that the stake awaits him, or the pilot who remains at the controls of his aeroplane to avoid crashing into a school? Depending on how we classify these examples, our moral assessment can be very different. Rather than being associated with the stigma of suicide, the individuals in these examples may in fact be praised and even regarded as heroes. The fact remains, however, that they all freely chose a course of action that they knew would lead to their deaths.

Given the nuances that distinguish the different kinds of self-inflicted death, some commentators prefer to avoid pejorative terms like 'suicide' and speak instead of 'voluntary death'. Perhaps a separate category of 'altruistic suicide' is needed within this to encompass the examples cited above, and also one of 'religious suicide' for cases like that of Thich Quang Duc. In discussions of both suicide and euthanasia, misunderstandings often arise due to a failure to provide definitions and clarify the issues at stake. I will say more about the term 'euthanasia' and its various nuances later in this chapter, but since the word 'suicide' is engrained in our everyday language, I propose to retain it in the present discussion now that the reader has been alerted to the possible semantic pitfalls.

Self-immolation in Buddhism

When Thich Quang Duc dramatically ended his life in 1963, he was both an innovator and an imitator. His special form of self-immolation has since been copied worldwide. In the decades since his death in 1963, there have been between 1,000 and 3,000 deaths by burning, many directly or indirectly modelled on his act. Vietnam accounts for by far the largest number, with some 23% of the total, representing 70 deaths. Next come India (16%), South Korea (14%) and the USA (9%). Most of the people who burn themselves as an act of public protest are young men, typically aged about 25. Many are students.

Thich Quang Duc was not the originator of the dramatic act he performed in Saigon, and as imitator stands at the end of a long tradition of self-immolation in East Asian Buddhism. The Vietnamese form of Buddhism is something of a hybrid, having been exposed to both Mahāyāna and Theravāda influences, but the strongest influence came from China to the north. In China there are many historical precedents for individuals burning either themselves or parts of their bodies for religious reasons. Burning of the body in a token way has formed part of the monastic ordination ritual in China and Korea down to modern times. In the course of the ordination ceremony a small cone of incense is placed on the monk's shaven head and ignited. When it burns away, it leaves a permanent mark on the scalp. Other, more dramatic, examples feature in the historical records, including burning off fingers or entire limbs (usually the arms), and in extreme cases burning the whole body. A 10th-century treatise by the Chinese monk Yongming Yanshou (904–75) commends these practices to ordinary monks and nuns (other authorities disagreed, arguing that such extreme acts were only appropriate for great bodhisattvas). Such deeds were seen by those who approved of them as sacrifices to the Buddha, recalling the master's own cremation, and demonstrating great piety and devotion.

The *Brahmajāla Sūtra* (*Fan Wang Ching*)

A Chinese text from the 5th century CE, this explains how new bodhisattvas should be instructed by one who knows the scriptures and regulations of the Mahāyāna:

> In accordance with the Dharma he should explain to them all the ascetic practices, such as setting fire to the body, setting fire to the arm, or setting fire to the finger. If one does not set fire to the body, the arm or the finger as an offering to the Buddhas, one is not a renunciant bodhisattva. Moreover, one should sacrifice the feet, hands and flesh of the body as offerings to hungry tigers, wolves, and lions and to all hungry ghosts.

It is interesting, however, as James Benn has shown, that the two texts that seem to validate these practices (the *Brahmajāla Sūtra* and the *Śūraṃgamasamādhi Sūtra*) are both apocryphal Chinese compositions, and neither has an Indian ancestor. Auto-cremation, furthermore, has ancient roots in China in the practice of moxibustion (the igniting of a cauterizing cone of herbs or other substances placed in contact with the body) and in ceremonies designed to produce rain. The Buddhist pedigree of these fiery suicides is therefore open to question.

Suicide has also been common in neighbouring Japan in the ritualized form that goes by the name of *seppuku* (it is also known as 'hara kiri', a more vulgar term meaning 'to slice the abdomen'). This act involves making two small crosswise slices across the gut while in a kneeling position, after which an assistant would behead the samurai with a sword (in practice the first step was rarely carried out). Beginning in the Tokugawa period, samurai warriors came to see this sacrifice as the penalty for a failure in their duty and as something enjoined by their professional code of honour. In modern times, large numbers of suicides occurred among the Japanese military in the wake of the country's defeat in the Second World War. Since many samurai turned to Buddhism, some commentators have come to see suicide as legitimized by Buddhist teachings, and have gone so far as to claim that the practice of suicide was approved of by the Buddha. We need to examine these claims and consider to what extent the East Asian practices described so far have a foundation in the early teachings.

Suicide in Indian Buddhism

The notion that suicide is permitted in Buddhism has gained currency largely because of a small number of well-known cases in the Pāli canon when monks who were sick and in pain took their own lives and apparently received a posthumous endorsement from the Buddha. Three cases are particularly important, those of the monks Channa, Vakkali, and Godhika. A special feature of these cases is that the monks in question attained *arhat*ship as they died and were not reborn. Because of this, something a consensus has emerged among scholars that while Buddhism is generally opposed to suicide it is prepared to make an exception in the case of the enlightened, since they in some sense or other have transcended conventional moral norms. This view was first put forward in the 1920s and since then has enjoyed broad support, although without having been subject to much critical examination. Having recently reviewed these cases myself, however, I have come to a rather different conclusion. My reading of the sources is that although the Buddha appears to have felt great sympathy for those involved, there is little evidence that he ever condoned suicide. His general position seems to have been that suicide is wrong, but that we should not judge too harshly those who take their own lives in circumstances of great pain or distress. However, there are alternative interpretations. One early school (the Sarvāstivāda) seems to have supported the view that suicide may be permitted to avoid loss of *arhat* status, and we are also told that the Buddha renounced his 'life principle' (*āyusaṃskāra*) three months before he died (D.ii.106) (whether this constitutes 'suicide' would seem to involve definitional problems of the kind described earlier).

Apart from these problematic cases relating to the special category of the enlightened, there is little support for suicide elsewhere in the early sources, and in general it is strongly discouraged. For example, when the monk Channa declares that he is contemplating 'using the knife' to end his suffering, the reaction of the *arhat* Śāriputra is to dissuade him in the strongest terms:

> Let the venerable Channa not use the knife! Let the venerable Channa live – we want the venerable Channa to live! If he lacks suitable food, I will go in search of suitable food for him. If he lacks suitable medicine, I will go in search of suitable medicine for him. If he lacks a proper attendant, I will attend on him. Let the venerable Channa not use the knife! Let the venerable Channa live – we want the venerable Channa to live!
>
> (M.iii.264)

These comments reflect the broad position of the early tradition, namely that acts of violence should be avoided and death should never be caused intentionally, even when it is one's own life that is in question.

One of the few places where suicide is discussed in some detail is in the Vinaya under the rubric of the third *pārājika*, the rule prohibiting the taking of human life. This rule has already been mentioned several times, including in the discussion of abortion in the previous chapter. The circumstances in which the rule was introduced have a direct bearing on suicide and also euthanasia. The commentary to the third *pārājika* relates how on one occasion the Buddha gave instruction to the monks on a specific form of meditation known as 'contemplation of the impure'. This is a method used to counteract attachment. In practising it, one reflects upon the body as impermanent, a thing subject to decay and corruption, and not a proper object of attachment. Having instructed the monks on this theme, the Buddha retired into seclusion for a fortnight. Unfortunately, the monks became overzealous in their practice and developed disgust and loathing for their bodies. So intense did this become that many felt death would be preferable to such a repulsive existence. Accordingly, they proceeded to kill themselves, and lent assistance to one another in doing so. They found a willing assistant in the form of Migalaṇḍika, a 'sham recluse' (*samaṇa-kuttaka*), who agreed to assist by killing the monks in return for their robes and bowls. Migalaṇḍika dispatched his victims with a large knife, killing a large number of monks, up to 60 on a single day. When the Buddha came out of his fortnight's seclusion, he noticed the drop in numbers among the monks and enquired as to the cause. When he learned what had taken place, he proclaimed the third *pārājika*. This episode shows the Buddha directly intervening to prevent monks committing suicide either by their own hand or with the assistance of others, and gives grounds for thinking that this reflects the normative Buddhist position.

The third *pārājika*, the monastic rule prohibiting taking human life

Should any monk intentionally deprive a human being of life or look about so as to be his knife-bringer, or eulogise death, or incite [anyone] to death saying 'My good man, what need have you of this evil, difficult life? Death would be better for you than life' – or who should deliberately and purposefully in various ways eulogise death or incite anyone to death: he is also one who is defeated, he is not in communion.

(Vin.iii.72)

It will be noted that the rule the Buddha introduced prohibits assisting others to commit suicide, not suicide itself. The reason for this is likely to be the technical one that the monastic rules are drawn up with a view to imposing appropriate sanctions and penalties on those who break them. In the case of a person who has killed himself, this question clearly does not arise.

It appears that the dramatic cases of suicide by auto-cremation we have discussed have no antecedents in the early tradition, and that the East Asian practices of self-immolation and *seppuku* originated outside Buddhism and have their roots in the indigenous cultures. This would seem to be confirmed by the example of Tibet, a region where practices such as ritual suicide and auto-cremation are not found. While these facts do not by themselves mean that suicide is immoral, it does make it difficult to claim that it has any foundation in the early teachings or was approved of by the Buddha. The general tenor of the early teachings, with their strong emphasis on non-violence, seems at odds with the kind of self-mutilation and destruction of the human body practised in parts of East Asia.

Euthanasia

The discussion of assisted suicide in the third *pārājika* leads naturally to the issue of euthanasia. By 'euthanasia' here is meant intentionally causing the death of a patient by act or omission in the context of medical care. We will confine our discussion to *voluntary* euthanasia, that is, when a mentally competent patient freely requests medical help in ending his or her life. Two principal modes of euthanasia are commonly distinguished, namely active and passive. Active euthanasia is the deliberate killing of a patient by an act, for example by lethal injection. Passive euthanasia is the intentional causing of death by omission, for example by failing to provide food, medicine, or some other requisite for life. Some commentators see this distinction as morally significant, whereas others do not. Given the importance Buddhism places on intention in moral evaluation, it would seem to matter little whether the fatal outcome is achieved by active or passive means. Note that on the definition in use here the borderline case of administering painkillers – which may simultaneously hasten death – does not count as euthanasia of either kind, since the doctor's intention in such circumstances is to kill the pain, not the patient.

There is no term synonymous with 'euthanasia' in early Buddhist sources, nor is the morality of the practice discussed in a systematic way. Given that monks were active as medical practitioners, however, circumstances occasionally arose when the value of life was called into question. These circumstances are outlined in certain of the case histories preserved in the Vinaya. In the 60 or so cases reported under this rubric, about one-third are concerned with deaths that occurred following medical intervention of one kind or another by monks. In some of these cases, the death of a patient was thought desirable for 'quality of life' reasons such as the avoidance of protracted terminal care (Vin.ii.79) or to minimize the suffering of patients with serious disabilities.

We have already considered the circumstances and provisions of the third *pārājika*, and this precept is particularly important in the context of euthanasia since the weight of the case for allowing euthanasia rests on the postulate that 'death would be better than life', especially when, to use the wording of the precept, life seems 'evil and difficult'. As noted, the precept is directed specifically at those who lend assistance to others in ending their lives, which the precept calls 'acting as knife-bringer'. This would seem to apply to all forms of euthanasia, and also physician-assisted suicide, in which the physician typically assists the person who wishes to die by prescribing lethal drugs, but crucially not administering them personally.

Compassion

As noted in Chapter 1, compassion is an important Buddhist moral value, and some sources reveal an increasing awareness of how a commitment to the alleviation of suffering can create a conflict with the principle of respect for life. Compassion, for example, might lead one to take life in order to alleviate suffering, and indeed is one of the main grounds on which euthanasia is commonly advocated.

The question of euthanasia performed for compassionate reasons (often called 'mercy killing') comes up in the Vinaya in the first of the cases to be reported after the precept against killing was declared (Vin.ii.79). In this case, the motive for bringing about the death of the patient is said to have been compassion (*karuṇā*) for the suffering of a dying monk. According to the commentator Buddhaghosa, those found guilty in this case took no direct action to terminate life but merely suggested to a dying monk that death would be preferable to his present condition.

Despite this apparently benevolent motive, namely to spare a dying person unnecessary pain, the judgement of the Buddha was that those involved were guilty of a breach of the precept. What had they done wrong? In Buddhaghosa's analysis the essence of their wrongdoing was that the guilty monks 'made death their aim' (*maraṇa-atthika*) (VA.ii.464). It would therefore appear immoral from a Buddhist perspective to embark on any course of action whose aim is the destruction of human life, regardless of the quality of the agent's motive. From this we may conclude that while compassion is always a morally good motive, it does not by itself justify whatever is done in its name.

Another important moral principle often invoked in the debate on euthanasia is autonomy. This involves the twin claims that the free choices of rational individuals should be respected, and that every individual has the right to dispose of his or her life as he or she sees fit. Buddhism would agree with this principle up to a point, since the doctrine of karma teaches that individuals have free will and are responsible for their moral choices. However, it also seems to want to place some limit on the scope of this freedom, as can be seen from the circumstances of the third *pārājika*. The monks involved here were, as far as we can tell, competent, rational adults. They wished to die because they had made the judgement that their lives were not worth living and that they would be better off dead. This was a free choice consequent upon their evaluation of their quality of life, which they deemed to be insufficient to justify continued existence. In terms of respect for autonomy, therefore, their decision might be thought justifiable, in the sense that as competent adults it was up to them to dispose of their lives as they saw fit. It seems, however, that the Buddha did not agree.

Must life be preserved at all costs?

Does the foregoing mean that Buddhism teaches that life must be preserved at all costs? At one point in his commentary, Buddhaghosa has a brief but interesting discussion about the situation of terminally ill patients in which two contrasting scenarios are mentioned. This is what he says:

Buddhist Ethics

> If one who is sick ceases to take food with the intention of dying when medicine and nursing care are at hand, he commits a minor offence (*dukkaṭa*). But in the case of a patient who has suffered a long time with a serious illness the nursing monks may become weary and turn away in despair thinking 'when will we ever cure him of this illness?' Here it is legitimate to decline food and medical care if the patient sees that the monks are worn out and his life cannot be prolonged even with intensive care.

(VA.ii.467)

The contrast here appears to be between the person who rejects medical care with the express purpose of ending his life, and one who resigns himself to the inevitability of death after treatment has failed and the medical resources have been exhausted. The moral distinction is that the first patient seeks death or 'makes death his aim', to use Buddhaghosa's phrase, while the second simply accepts the proximity and inevitability of death and rejects further treatment or nourishment as pointless. The first patient wishes to die; the second wishes to live but is resigned to the fact that he is beyond medical help.

The scenario described by Buddhaghosa suggests that Buddhism does not believe there is a moral obligation to preserve life at all costs. Recognizing the inevitability of death, of course, is a central element in Buddhist teachings. Death cannot be postponed forever, and Buddhists are encouraged to be mindful and prepared for the evil hour when it comes. To seek to prolong life beyond its natural span by recourse to ever-more elaborate technology when no cure or recovery is in sight is a denial of the reality of human mortality and would be seen by Buddhism as arising from delusion (*moha*) and excessive attachment (*tṛṣṇā*).

Following this line of reasoning, in terminal care situations, including those in which patients have been conclusively diagnosed as being in a 'persistent vegetative state', there would be no need to go to extreme lengths to provide treatment when there is little or no prospect of recovery. There would thus be no requirement to treat subsequent complications, for example pneumonia or other infections, by administering antibiotics. While it might be foreseen that an untreated infection would lead to the patient's death, it would also be recognized that any course of treatment that is contemplated must be assessed against the background of the overall prognosis for recovery. Rather than embarking on a series of piecemeal treatments, none of which would produce a net improvement in the patient's overall condition, it would often be appropriate to reach the conclusion that the patient was beyond medical help and let events to take their course. It is also justifiable to refuse or withdraw treatment that is either futile or too burdensome in the light of the overall condition.

Conclusion

There is a traditional view in Buddhism that the human lifespan is determined by karma, and that accordingly death will come at the appointed time. To shorten life artificially through suicide or euthanasia is seen by many Buddhists as tampering or interfering with one's destiny. As regards suicide, people take their own lives for many reasons, and we need to know something of the motivation and circumstances involved before making a judgement. There is a world of difference between the tragic suicide of a depressed teenager and the altruistic self-immolation of a Thich Quang Duc.

In the context of terminal care, it is widely felt that it is preferable to allow events to take their natural course rather than resorting to euthanasia to shorten life. Not all Buddhists agree, however, and some, particularly in the West, see Buddhism as allowing its followers the freedom to choose the time and manner of their death in the way they see fit. The arguments here reflect those found in the broader debate on euthanasia currently taking place in many countries. Euthanasia has been legalized in the Netherlands and in Belgium, and no doubt Buddhists in these and other countries have found themselves on opposite sides of the debate. Just as Chinese Buddhists in the 10th century disagreed on whether it was right to burn limbs, so Buddhists today may differ on the morality of suicide and euthanasia.

That said, there appears to be no strong demand for the legalization of euthanasia by Buddhists. Few, if any, Buddhist groups have campaigned for it, and euthanasia has not been made legal in any Buddhist country. Rather than seek to introduce euthanasia as an option in terminal care, it seems most Buddhists would support the ideals of the hospice movement. In the West, the San Francisco Zen Center has offered facilities for the dying since 1971, and started a full-scale training programme for hospice workers in 1987. In 1986, the Buddhist Hospice Trust was founded in the UK. Not itself a hospice, this organization exists to explore Buddhist thinking on matters relating to death, dying, and bereavement. It also provides access to a network of volunteers who visit the dying and bereaved at their request. Buddhism has a great openness about death and encourages its followers to meditate on it and prepare for it in practical ways. The death of the Buddha is the example most Buddhists would seek to emulate. Despite being 80 years old and having suffered various painful illnesses in the last months of his life, he faced death mindfully and serenely. As always, he thought more of others than himself: only after giving his disciples a final opportunity to ask questions and clear up any remaining doubts about his teachings did he enter final nirvana.

Chapter 8
Cloning

The birth of Dolly the sheep caused a furore when it was announced to the world on 24 February 1997. What made this birthday so special was that Dolly was unlike any other sheep, not solely because she had been created by scientists in the laboratories of the Roslin Institute in Edinburgh, but because she had been produced by means of a new technology that threatens to revolutionize the way we think about the basis of life itself. Since the 1950s scientists had been experimenting with cloning tadpoles and frogs, but Dolly was the first mammalian clone, and her genetic proximity to the human species gave cause for deep reflection and concern as the implications for human beings were assessed. Dolly has since been followed by cloned mice, goats, pigs, cats, and horses, and it seems only a matter of time until the technique is perfected for use on human beings. It is in connection with this prospect – chilling to some and exciting to others – that profound moral issues arise.

Some scientists and experts in fertility research have declared themselves in favour of human cloning and are actively pursuing experiments to perfect the technique. Others have claimed that the taboo has already been broken. The Raelian religious cult claimed that a first cloned child – significantly named Eve – was delivered by Caesarean section on 26 December 2002. The group went on to make further claims, including the birth of a second cloned child in the Netherlands to a lesbian couple in early January 2003, a third birth in late January to a Japanese couple who had cloned their dead son, and another to a couple from Saudi Arabia. None of these claims has been verified, and the scientific community remains highly sceptical. The Raelians, founded by French journalist Claude Vorilhon (now called Rael), are enthusiastic about cloning because of their belief that humans were created by extraterrestrials and that Jesus was resurrected through an advanced cloning technique. They hold that the soul dies when the body dies, and therefore see cloning as the way to personal immortality. 'Once we can clone exact replicas of ourselves', their publicity proclaims, 'the next step will be to transfer our memory and personality into our newly cloned brains, which will allow us to truly live forever.'

Conventional research teams have claimed more modest success. In 2001, US-based Advanced Cell Technology claimed to have produced the world's first cloned embryos, but none grew beyond six cells, and in February 2004 a team in South Korea announced that it had grown 30 cloned embryos to the blastocyst stage, when the embryo is a tiny ball of 100 to 150 cells. A member of the team, Professor Yong Moon from Korea's Seoul National University, was quoted in news reports as saying, 'Cloning is a different way of thinking about the recycling of life – it's a Buddhist way of thinking.' Whether one accepts this opinion or not, cloning is not a simple technique, and the successful birth of Dolly was preceded by 276 failed attempts. Human cloning may prove to be even more difficult, and the world may not awake to another shock announcement quite as soon as some expect.

The science of cloning

A clone is a genetic duplicate – a kind of photocopy – of another individual. The word 'clone' is from the Greek *klon*, meaning a twig, and the idea of cloning resembles the way horticulturalists take cuttings from a mature plant and grow them into identical copies of their parent. Cloning in human beings replaces the normal process of sexual intercourse. Instead of an ovum being fertilized by a sperm, the nucleus of an unfertilized ovum is removed and replaced with a nucleus of a somatic (body) cell from a donor (a skin cell is typically used for this purpose). The ovum is then stimulated and its cells begin to divide and reduplicate as in a normal embryo. The developing embryo is placed in the womb and develops into an individual with the same genetic make-up as the donor of the cell nucleus. Since the technique involves the transfer of the nucleus of a somatic cell to an embryo, the cloning technique goes by the scientific name of 'Somatic Cell Nuclear Transfer', or SCNT.

In conventional reproduction, each parent contributes 23 of the 46 chromosomes that will determine the child's genetic identity. A cloned child, however, inherits all 46 of its chromosomes from a single DNA source. The social relation of a clone to its parent is problematic. The nearest parallel in genetic terms is that of identical twins, since both individuals have the same DNA pattern in each somatic cell. However, there would be a difference in the ages of the clone and its progenitor, since the latter would be much older, normally an adult, and here the parallel with identical twins begins to break down and the relationship starts to look more like one of parent and child. Other problems and conundrums surround the relationship between the cloned infant and the people who participate in its creation and nurture. Up to three 'mothers' could play a part, as shown in Figure 10, namely: the donor of the unfertilized egg cell; the woman in whose womb the cloned embryo is implanted (the foster mother); the person (who could also be male) who contributes the somatic cell from which the DNA is extracted and placed in the enucleated egg cell. The legal and emotional traumas that could result from a scenario in which three women lay claim to the title of 'mother' would keep the courts and psychotherapists busy for years.

The type of cloning envisaged in Figure 10 is known as 'reproductive cloning'. The aim of this procedure is to produce a baby, perhaps a baby sheep, as in the case of Dolly, or a human baby. An alternative type of cloning procedure is known as 'therapeutic cloning'. Here

Reproductive cloning

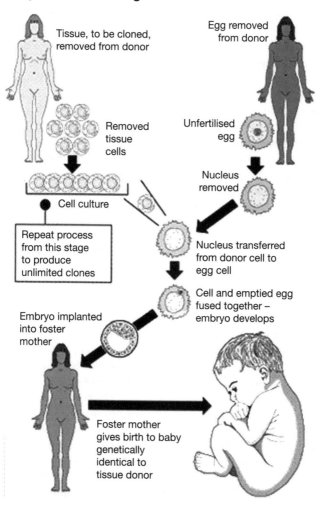

Tissue, to be cloned, removed from donor

Egg removed from donor

Removed tissue cells

Unfertilised egg

Cell culture

Nucleus removed

Repeat process from this stage to produce unlimited clones

Nucleus transferred from donor cell to egg cell

Cell and emptied egg fused together – embryo develops

Embryo implanted into foster mother

Foster mother gives birth to baby genetically identical to tissue donor

10. Reproductive cloning

the purpose is not to produce a living copy of an individual, but to carry out experimentation on early embryos as part of a programme of scientific research. The broad aim of this research is to better understand the process of genetic development in order to prevent abnormalities and to develop treatments using gene therapy to alleviate chronic hereditary diseases, such as Huntingdon's disease and cystic fibrosis. Treatments of this kind, which are known as somatic therapies, work by targeting and repairing genetically abnormal cells, for example by introducing missing genes. When the aim is to modify the reproductive cells (sperm and ova) so as to cure hereditary diseases, the treatment is known as 'germ-line' therapy. Such treatments raise additional moral issues since they modify not only the DNA of the individual patient but also that of any offspring. There are great risks involved with this therapy, since tinkering with the genetic legacy of an individual may blight the lives of future generations. Indeed, because its effects are unforeseeable, many commentators believe that the risks involved in germ-line therapy are too great. On the other hand, supporters claim that although the risks are great, so too are the potential benefits; the prospect of freeing future offspring from the misery of an inherited disease tips the balance for some in favour of the treatment.

Many researchers believe that special cells called stem cells have an important role to play in the development of genetic therapies. Stem cells, which begin to appear in the embryo at the blastocyst stage, have the ability to divide for indefinite periods in culture and to give rise to other more specialized cells. Because of the power they have to grow into any kind of somatic cell – such as a brain cell, a liver cell, a heart or blood cell – they are described as 'pluripotent'. This means they function a bit like the joker in a pack of playing cards, which can take on any value as the context requires. The stem cells used in research are obtained from two main sources, the first being excess embryos left over after infertility treatment. Here, the inner cell mass of the embryo, which contains the pluripotent cells, is cultured to produce a pluripotent stem cell line. The second method is to isolate pluripotent stem cells from fetal tissue obtained from terminated pregnancies, and here we encounter dilemmas familiar from the discussion of abortion in Chapter 6. Since in these cases an abortion will already have been carried out, and the cells to be used would otherwise simply be destroyed along with the fetal remains, some observers feel that there is nothing immoral in the use of this tissue for scientific research. Others consider that the research itself is tainted by its association with the abortion, even when this was carried out in accordance with legal requirements, the consent of the mother was obtained, and the research holds the promise of alleviating suffering.

Stem cells are also found in adults (for example, stem cells reside in the bone marrow and perform the critical role of replenishing our supply of blood cells) and recent experiments have shown that these may retain a greater capacity to diversify than had hitherto been thought. If adult cells can be utilized, an important objection to stem cell research could be removed, but as yet the flexibility of adult stem cells has only been observed in animals and in limited tissue types.

The view one comes to regarding stem cell research will be influenced by the view one takes on abortion, and although, as we have seen, traditional Buddhist teachings oppose abortion, in practice Buddhists are as likely to be as divided on this question as any other group.

Cloning and IVF

Cloning could conceivably have a role to play in connection with *in vitro* fertilization (IVF). When the husband is infertile, he could act as DNA donor, providing a skin cell instead of a sex cell. The DNA would be inserted into an ovum provided by the wife, and the result would be a child who was genetically identical to the father but who was carried to term in the womb of its non-genetic mother. Such a situation may be less than ideal, since parents normally wish their child to have a genetic similarity to them both, but as a last resort the outcome may not be totally unacceptable. At least it provides a child who strongly resembles one of the parents, will be carried by the mother in her womb as in a normal pregnancy, and will also inherit some DNA (the mitochondrial DNA surrounding the nucleus of the egg cell) from its mother. For many infertile couples, this may be a more acceptable solution than childlessness or adoption. Other scenarios in which cloning may play a part include providing children for lesbian couples (one partner donates the ovum and the other the DNA), or in cases when a woman wishes to conceive a child after the death of her partner using his genetic material.

The kinds of examples just described are both rare and controversial, and it is unlikely that cloning would have a major role to play as an adjunct to IVF programmes. We have already mentioned the risky and unproven nature of the cloning procedure, and until such risks were reduced to an acceptable level, there could be no question of contemplating cloning human beings. Dolly the sheep had to be put down in February 2002 after developing arthritis and suffering from progressive lung disease, and many cloned fetuses exhibit 'giantism', a condition in which they grow so large that the womb cannot contain them.

Objections to cloning

In the furore that followed the birth of Dolly, cloning met with widespread condemnation by churchmen and politicians from across the globe. The reaction was so strong that many countries introduced legislation or took other measures to deter or prohibit human cloning. The United States prohibited the use of federal funds for cloning research, and in the UK the Human Reproductive Cloning Act (2001) made it illegal to implant a cloned embryo in a woman (although allowing cloning experiments to be carried out on embryos up to 14 days). Cloning was made illegal in France, Germany, and Japan, and in Australia the Gene Technology Act

2000 was introduced to regulate the procedure. In this general wave of disapproval, religious opposition was led by the theistic traditions, notably Christianity, Judaism, and Islam. These religions teach that life is a gift from God, and for them the creation of life in the laboratory seems to usurp the divine authority of the creator. The Bible teaches that God created human beings in his image by breathing life into the bodies he formed from clay, and to seek to duplicate this miracle in a laboratory seems to some an act of great hubris. Reproductive cloning is also in conflict with the biblical model of sexual generation. We are told in the Book of Genesis that God created human beings 'male and female' and enjoined them to multiply through sexual union, a practice which subsequent Christian authorities regard as appropriate only within the constraints of marriage. Cloning respects none of these religious precedents, and in the eyes of many believers threatens to undermine divinely sanctioned norms governing family and social life.

Many of these theological objections disappear when cloning is viewed from a Buddhist perspective. Since Buddhism does not believe in a supreme being, there is no divine creator who might be offended by human attempts to duplicate his work. Nor does Buddhism believe in a personal soul, or teach that human beings are made in God's image. Its view of creation and cosmology is very different from that of the Bible, and does not seem to carry with it any normative principles or obligations relating to reproduction. There is no theological reason, then, why cloning could not be seen as just another way of creating life, neither intrinsically better nor worse than any other.

The objection that cloning involves 'playing God' in the literal sense (by creating life) goes hand in hand with a similar objection to playing God in a metaphorical sense. Such objections depict the creator of the clone as having godlike powers over the creature he has given life to, to the extent of controlling virtually every aspect of its development. The parallel with the story of Frankenstein has been drawn by several commentators who see cloning as based on a 'producer-product' type of relationship rather than one of respect for the equal dignity of human beings. Critics such as Jeremy Rifkin claim that a cloned child would be denied an 'open future' because the child would be made in the image and likeness of an already existing individual as opposed to having its own unique genetic code. Other commentators, such as Bryan Appleyard, fear that cloning could lead to a revival of eugenics programmes that aim to produce 'a better race of men', and in due course to the kind of society depicted in the film *Gattaca* in which genetics determines every detail of an individual's life from the cradle to the grave.

Supporters of cloning regard such concerns as overstated, and point out that clones have been with us throughout history in the form of identical twins. The fact that two individuals share the same genetic code, they say, has never threatened the fabric of society. Furthermore, just as identical twins differ (for example in the curvature of the skull and the shape of internal organs), an individual produced by cloning would be only a fuzzy copy of the DNA donor. There are several reasons for this. Even with identical DNA, there are underlying differences at the molecular level which will become greater as the clone develops. The DNA supplied by the mother (mitochondrial DNA) can also subtly alter the overall genetic 'mix'. Another important reason is that the development of an individual brain is always a unique process, and while DNA may determine the rough layout of the wiring, it cannot control the operation of trillions of neurons and synapses. Environmental factors also play an important part in individual development, and have a profoundly formative influence on personality, perhaps even greater than that of DNA. Each individual undergoes a different set of experiences over the course of a lifetime, and these experiences shape character and personality, making every individual unique. No two individuals are ever the same, regardless of their DNA, and the fear of armies of identical, mindless clones being directed by evil dictators is therefore more a product of science fiction than scientific fact. For one thing, it is hard to see where the egg cells to produce the clones would come from. There is already a serious shortage of eggs for IVF programmes, and in the context of resource allocation ethics committees may feel that the treatment of existing cases of infertility takes priority over unproven and possibly wasteful cloning experiments. Some of the fears that have been expressed about cloning may accordingly be overstated. Even if this is the case, however, the advent of cloning is likely to influence our view of human nature and the concept of human dignity in complex ways, and the warnings of the objectors merit serious consideration by laymen and scientists alike.

Cloning and Buddhist teachings

Who's Afraid of Human Cloning by Gregory E. Pence was one of the first books to make a positive case for human cloning. Pence began his book with the following quotation.

> Buddhist scholar Donald Lopez foresees real problems for the theory of karma. Would the clone inherit the karma of the original person? And he wonders 'What did the sheep do in a previous life that resulted in its being cloned in this one?'

The belief in karma introduces many conundrums and complexities of this kind, since both karma and DNA may be thought to account for how people come to be born with specific physical and mental characteristics. Which is correct: Buddhism or science? Other puzzling questions also arise, such as 'Is it possible to clone a Buddha?', and 'Is there a Buddha gene?'. For the remainder of the chapter, I will explore some of these intriguing questions.

When considering the possibility of cloning a Buddha, the starting point of our speculations must be whether or not the Buddha had a normal physical human body or whether in some way he transcended the conventional laws of nature, including those of genetics. While the Theravāda school holds that the Buddha was an ordinary mortal, within a few centuries of his death certain schools

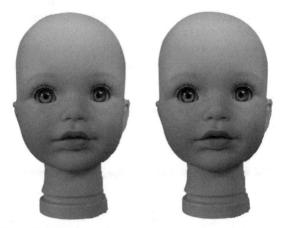

11. If scientists can clone a baby . . .

12. . . . could they clone a Buddha?

(notably the Sarvāstivāda) came to regard him more and more as a supernatural being who in addition to his physical body (*rūpakāya*) was also endowed with a magical body capable of miraculous transformation (this is like the kind of ethereal body that angels in Christianity are thought to possess). Notions of this kind were eventually formalized in later Mahāyāna Buddhism in the doctrine of the Buddha's 'three bodies' (*trikāya*). In this scheme, the earthly body was known as his Emanation Body (*nirmāṇakāya*), his magical body was termed his Enjoyment Body (*saṃbhogakāya*), and the last and most sublime of the three was said to be his Truth Body (*dharmakāya*). We do not need to go into abstruse questions of Buddhology here, but it is important to realize that for many believers the Buddha was always more than a simple human being, and that even his Emanation Body was (as the name suggests) more a kind of magical projection than a flesh-and-blood reality. Even the Theravāda school teaches that the Buddha's body bore 32 distinctive 'marks' (*lakṣaṇa*) that identified his as the body of a 'great man' (*mahāpuruṣa*). These marks include a number of extraordinary attributes (for example, the mark of a wheel on the soles of his feet, and web-like skin between his fingers and toes). We are also told in this list of features that the Buddha had 40 teeth (instead of the normal 32) and that he had blue eyes. When discussing the possibility of cloning the Buddha, the first problem, then, is to decide which of the foregoing 'bodies' of the Buddha would be the one to be cloned. For the sake of simplicity, I propose to avoid all reference to supernatural bodies here, and to proceed on the assumption that the Buddha's physical body was of the human kind known to science.

So, would it be possible to clone one Buddha and produce another Buddha? Since we are assuming that the Buddha had human DNA, there seems no reason why he could not be cloned, perhaps using DNA from a relic. The result would be a genetic duplicate similar to the kind seen in the case of identical twins, with the difference that one Buddha (the DNA donor) would be an adult and the other (the clone) a baby. As the clone grew to adulthood, we would expect to see a striking physical resemblance to the donor. The interesting question, however, is whether the resemblance would be purely a physical one or whether the clone would also be an enlightened being. The answer to this question depends on the view we take as to whether enlightenment is a function of DNA. It seems at least plausible that a number of personal attributes and capacities are determined by DNA. Strength and athletic prowess, for instance, seem to be determined by hereditary factors, as does intelligence. As every teacher knows, children with a high IQ generally learn more quickly. Being intelligent, however, is not the same as being enlightened. By enlightenment (*bodhi*), Buddhists understand not just physical or mental capacities but the development of those capacities in a particular way. Buddhas, for example, are thought to have a profound insight (*prajñā*) into the nature of things, including a deep understanding of important truths about human nature (such as that it lacks a self) and of the nature of the world we live in (such as that all phenomena are dependently originated). So far as I am aware, no geneticist would suggest that specific concepts, truths, or propositions of this kind are encoded in the structure of DNA. It is difficult to see, then, how there could be anything like a 'Buddha gene' which could serve as the genetic marker for enlightenment. We know from the Buddha's life story that his enlightenment was not the product of his birth, but the result of lifetimes of spiritual practice. The possession of a 'Buddha gene' would have rendered all this unnecessary. It also follows that if enlightenment was a genetic trait, those who lacked the appropriate DNA would forever be excluded from attaining the goal of Buddhahood. It seems, then, that Buddha's are made, not born. Cloning a Buddha, accordingly, would result in close physical duplicates, somewhat like the famous 'doubles' used by Saddam Hussein to avoid assassination. Although they all resembled him, however, only one was the real dictator of Iraq.

There is, however, another possibility, that DNA itself is somehow modified from one lifetime to the next under the influence of karma. The Buddha explained the various differences among individuals as being due to karma, making a specific link between lifespan (*āyus*), illness (*ābādha*), physical appearance (*varṇa*), and intellectual ability (*prajñā*) (M.iii.202f). Since we now know that such characteristics are to a great extent determined by DNA, does this mean that karma exerts an influence on DNA predisposing individuals in the ways mentioned? This seems unlikely, since, as we saw in Chapter 6, Buddhism has always taught that the material basis of human life is supplied entirely by one's parents through the union of the male and female genetic components which give rise to a new individual. Karma plays no part in this biological process, of which genetics has given a perfectly satisfactory account. The individual human genome is entirely determined by parental DNA, and since the parents pre-exist the child it is impossible that the karma of an as yet unconceived child could modify the DNA it inherits. There seem to be only two ways karma can influence DNA. The first is indirectly, by directing the individual being reborn to a particular set of parents with a certain kind of DNA. This, indeed, is how rebirth is represented as taking place in many Buddhist traditions, which portray the spirit seeking rebirth (*gandharva*) as attracted by the erotic activity of its parents-to-be and driven by the desire and the affinity it feels for them to enter the womb of its mother while intercourse is taking place. The second possibility is that karma directly influences the particular genetic pattern the parental sex cells adopt when they fuse. It is evident that brothers and sisters may share the same parental DNA but may vary greatly in physical appearance as well as being of different genders, and it may be that karma exerts some influence over the as yet not well understood mechanism which determines the individual DNA coding that will be produced when sperm and ovum unite. This second explanation seems unlikely, and many researchers believe it is only a matter of time until science provides an explanation of how an individual's DNA pattern is produced at conception, thereby making a karmic explanation redundant.

If, as I have suggested, karma has no direct connection to DNA, we have an answer to the question raised by Donald Lopez above as to whether a cloned individual would inherit the karma of the DNA donor. The answer is no: a clone would no more share the karma of its DNA donor than one identical twin shares the karma of the other. It seems axiomatic in Buddhist teachings that karma is personal to each individual and that no two individuals can share the same karma (in effect, this would mean they were the same person). Thus, although karma and DNA may produce similar results, they are separate mechanisms and there is no causal link between them.

Conclusion

What conclusions can be drawn about the ethics of cloning from a Buddhist perspective? The first point to reiterate is that the technique itself need not be seen as theologically improper or immoral: cloning is just another way of creating human life. IVF programmes have created 'test-tube babies' since 1968, and the fact that fertilization takes place in the laboratory rather than in the bedroom does not appear to have resulted in any serious harm to the children born through the technique.

As regards therapeutic (as opposed to reproductive) cloning, however, Buddhism is likely to have strong reservations. Creating human life only to destroy it in the course of experimentation, for example by harvesting stem cells, is directly contrary to the principle of *ahiṃsā*. Regardless of the benevolent motivation for such experimentation (which also typically involves scientific curiosity and financial rewards), Buddhism would not sanction engaging in death-dealing experiments or accept the utilitarian moral logic of destroying one life to save another (or even many more). Quite apart from the problems surrounding the technique itself, cloning must also be subject to the same general moral standards that apply to any other human activity. This means that the motivation of those involved must be wholesome (free from greed, hatred, and delusion) and the reasonably foreseeable consequences for individuals and society at large must be taken into account. Many reservations have been expressed in the latter regard, from the erosion of human dignity to a return to the eugenics programmes of the 1930s and 1940s, and these fears cannot be dismissed lightly. On the other hand, few clear benefits to cloning human beings have been identified. Scientific curiosity seems to be the main factor motivating cloning experiments at present, and overall Buddhists are likely to be sceptical about the need for this curiosity to be satisfied at the price of destroying human life.

References

Chapter 1

M. Cone and R. Gombrich (tr.), *The Perfect Generosity of Prince Vessantara* (Oxford: Clarendon Press, 1977); K. Crosby and A. Skilton, *The Bodhicaryāvatāra* (Oxford: Oxford University Press, 1996).

Chapter 2

J. F. Fletcher, *Situation Ethics: The New Morality* (London: SCM Press, 1966); K. Jayatilleke, 'The Ethical Theory of Buddhism', *The Mahabodhi*, 78 (1970): 192–7; the *Journal of Buddhist Ethics* publishes online at *http://jbe.gold.ac.uk*; W. L. King, *In the Hope of Nibbana: The Ethics of Theravada Buddhism* (La Salle, Ill.: Open Court, 1964); P. D. Premasiri, 'Moral Evaluation in Early Buddhism', *Sri Lanka Journal of the Humanities*, 1 (1975): 63–74; Christopher Queen, *Engaged Buddhism in the West* (Boston: Wisdom, 2000); T. W. Rhys Davids, *The Questions of King Milinda* (London: Oxford University Press, 1925).

Chapter 3

Lynn White, Jr, 'The Historical Roots of Our Ecological Crisis', *Science*, vol. 155: 1203–7 (10 March 1967); on the 'hermit strand', see Lambert Schmithausen, 'The Early Buddhist Tradition and Ethics', *Journal of Buddhist Ethics* (*http://jbe.la.psu.edu/4/schm1.html*); the *Jīvaka Sutta* is available online at *http://www.accesstoinsight.org/canon/sutta/anguttara/an08-026.html*.

Chapter 4

For the *Abhidharmakośa-bhāṣya of Vasubandhu*, see L. de la Vallée Poussin, P. Pradhan, and S. Jha, *The Abhidharmakośa of Vasubandhu, with the Commentary* (Patna: K.P. Jayaswal Research Institute, 1983); sGam Po Pa and H. V. Guenther, *The Jewel Ornament of Liberation* (Boston: Shambhala, 1986), p. 76; Phra Pisarn Thammapatee's remarks on gay monks are reported at *http://www.floatinglotus.com/news/tnewsgaymonks.html*; on *paṇḍakas*, see P. Harvey, *An Introduction to Buddhist Ethics: Foundations, Values and Issues* (Cambridge: Cambridge University Press, 2000), p. 434; L. Zwilling is quoted in Harvey, p. 416; a report on the Dalai Lama's meeting with gay leaders is available at *http://www.shambhalasun.com/Archives/Features/1998/Mar98/Peskind.htm*; L. P. N. Perera, *Sexuality in Ancient India: A Study Based on the Pali Vinayapitaka* (Sri Lanka: University of Kelaniya, 1993), p. 234.

Chapter 5

Takuan quoted by P. Harvey, *An Introduction to Buddhist Ethics: Foundations, Values and Issues* (Cambridge: Cambridge University Press, 2000), p. 268; Harada Daiun Soogaku quoted in B. D. A. Victoria, *Zen at War* (New York and Tokyo: Weatherhill, 1998), p. 137; Yasutani Haku'un quoted by David Loy in a review of *Zen War Stories*, *Journal of Buddhist Ethics* (*http://jbe.gold.ac.uk/11/loy.html*); 'In infusing the suicidal Japanese military spirit . . . ', B. D. A. Victoria, *Zen War Stories* (London: Routledge Curzon, 2003), p. 144; Aung San Suu Kyi interview: *http://www.asiantribune.com*

Chapter 6

Bhikkhu Nyanamoli, *The Path of Purification* (Berkeley, Ca.: Shambhala Publications, 1976); *The lamp thoroughly illuminating the presentation of the three basic bodies – death, intermediate state and rebirth* by Yang-jen-ga-way-lo-drö, translated by Lati Rinbochay and J. Hopkins, *Death, Intermediate State and Rebirth in Tibetan Buddhism* (London: Rider, 1979), p. 62; Michael Barnhart, 'Buddhism and the Morality of Abortion', *Journal of Buddhist Ethics*, 5 (1998): 276–97 (*http://jbe.gold.ac.uk/5/barnh981.htm*); Mary Anne Warren, 'On the

Moral and Legal Status of Abortion', *The Monist*, vol. 57, no.1 (January 1973); abortion statistics quoted in Robert Florida, 'Buddhism and Abortion' in Damien Keown (ed.), *Contemporary Buddhist Ethics* (Richmond, Surrey: Curzon Press, 2000), pp. 137–68.

Chapter 7

D. Halberstam, *The Making of a Quagmire* (New York: Random House, 1965); Thich Nhat Hanh, *Vietnam: Lotus in a Sea of Fire* (New York: Hill and Wang, 1967); the *Brahmajāla Sūtra* is available only in French translation: J. J. M. de Groot, *La code du Mahāyāna en Chine* (New York: Garland Publishers, 1980); James Benn, 'Where Text Meets Flesh: Burning the Body as an "Apocryphal Practice" in Chinese Buddhism', *History of Religions* 37/4 (May 1998): 295–322; Damien Keown, 'Buddhism and Suicide: The Case of Channa', *Journal of Buddhist Ethics*, 3 (1996): 8–31; suicide statistics from Michael Biggs, 'Protest as Sacrifice: Self-Immolation in the Global Repertoire, 1963–2002': (*https://netfiles.uiuc.edu/biggsm/www/global.pdf*).

Chapter 8

The Raelian cult has a web page at *http://www.rael.org*; Professor Yong Moon, 'Buddhism at One with Stem Cell Research', *ABC Science Online* (*http://www.abc.net.au/science/news/stories/s1046974.htm*), 18 February 2004; Ted Howard and J. Rifkin, *Who Should Play God? The Artificial Creation of Life and What It Means for the Future of the Human Race* (New York: Dell Publishing Company, 1977); J. Rifkin, *The Biotech Century* (London: Phoenix, 1999); B. Appleyard, *Brave New Worlds: Genetics and the Human Experience* (London: HarperCollins, 2000); G. E. Pence, *Who's Afraid of Human Cloning?* (Lanham: Rowman and Littlefield, 1998).

Further reading

Chapter 1

P. Harvey, *An Introduction to Buddhist Ethics: Foundations, Values and Issues* (Cambridge: Cambridge University Press, 2000), chapters 1–3; J. Holt, *Discipline, the Canonical Buddhism of the Vinayapitaka* (Delhi: Motilal Banarsidass, 1981); P. Morgan and C. Lawton, *Ethical Issues in Six Religious Traditions* (Edinburgh: Edinburgh University Press, 1996); M. Pye, *Skilful Means: A Concept in Mahayana Buddhism* (London: Duckworth, 1978); H. Saddhatissa, *Buddhist Ethics* (Boston: Wisdom, 1997); L. Schmithausen, 'A Note on the Origins of *Ahiṃsā*', in *Harānandalaharī: Volume in Honour of Professor Minoru Hara on his Seventieth Birthday*, ed. R. Tsuchida and M. Hara (Reinbek: Verlag für Orientalistische Fachpublikationen, 2000); U. Tahtinen, *Ahiṃsā: Non-Violence in Indian Tradition* (London: Rider, 1976); Thanissaro Bhikkhu, *The Buddhist Monastic Code* (Metta Forest Monastery, Valley Center, CA, 1994); M. Wijayaratana, *Buddhist Monastic Life* (Cambridge: Cambridge University Press, 1990).

Chapter 2

S. Blackburn, *Ethics: A Very Short Introduction* (Oxford: Oxford University Press, 2003); W. K. Frankena, *Ethics* (Englewood Cliffs, NJ: Prentice-Hall, 1973); D. J. Fasching and D. Dechant (eds), *Comparative Religious Ethics: A Narrative Approach* (Oxford: Blackwell, 2001); R. Hindery, *Comparative Ethics in Hindu and Buddhist Traditions* (Delhi: Motilal Banarsidas, 1978); D. Little and S. B. Twiss,

Comparative Religious Ethics (San Francisco: Harper and Row, 1978); Damien Keown, *The Nature of Buddhist Ethics* (Basingstoke: Palgrave, 2001); G. S. P. Misra, *Development of Buddhist Ethics* (Delhi: Munshiram Manoharlal, 1984); J. Whitehill, 'Buddhism and the Virtues', in *Contemporary Buddhist Ethics*, ed. Damien Keown (Richmond, Surrey: Curzon Press, 2000); C. Hallisey, 'Ethical Particularism in Theravāda Buddhism', *Journal of Buddhist Ethics*, 3 (1996): 32–43; Christopher Queen, *Engaged Buddhism in the West* (Boston: Wisdom, 2000); Christopher Queen, Charles Prebish, and Damien Keown (eds), *Action Dharma: New Studies in Engaged Buddhism* (London: Routledge Curzon, 2003).

Chapter 3

A. H. Badiner, *Dharma Gaia: A Harvest of Essays in Buddhism and Ecology* (Berkeley, CA: Parallax Press, 1990); M. Batchelor and Kerry Brown (eds), *Buddhism and Ecology* (London: Cassell, 1992); Bodhipaksa, *Vegetarianism* (Birmingham: Windhorse, 1999); P. de Silva, *Environmental Philosophy and Ethics in Buddhism* (New York: St. Martin's Press, 1998); R. Epstein, Buddhist Resources on Vegetarianism and Animal Welfare (web resource): *http:// online.sfsu.edu/%7Erone/Buddhism/BuddhismAnimalsVegetarian/ BuddhistVegetarian.htm*; I. Harris, 'Buddhism and Ecology', in *Contemporary Buddhist Ethics*, ed. Damien Keown (Richmond, Surrey: Curzon Press, 2000); P. Harvey, *An Introduction to Buddhist Ethics: Foundations, Values and Issues* (Cambridge: Cambridge University Press, 2000), chapter 4; S. P. James, *Zen Buddhism and Environmental Ethics* (Aldershot: Ashgate, 2003); S. Kaza and K. Kraft, *Dharma Rain: Sources of Buddhist Environmentalism* (Boston, Mass.: Shambhala Publications, 2000); J. Macy, *World as Lover, World as Self* (Berkeley, CA: Parallax Press, 1991); A. Naess, *Ecology, Community and Lifestyle: Outline of an Ecosophy* (Cambridge: Cambridge University Press, 1990); K. Sandell (ed.), *Buddhist Perspectives on the Ecocrisis* (Kandy: Buddhist Publication Society, 1987); L. Schmithausen, 'The Early Buddhist Tradition and Ethics', *Journal of Buddhist Ethics* (*http:// jbe.la.psu.edu/4/schm1.html*); L. Schmithausen, 'Buddhism and the Ethics of Nature. Some Remarks', *The Eastern Buddhist*, New Series

XXXII (2000): 26–78; D. K. Swearer, 'Buddhism and Ecology: Challenge and Promise', *http://environment.harvard.edu/religion/ religion/buddhism*; M. E. Tucker and D. R. Williams, *Buddhism and Ecology: The Interconnection of Dharma and Deeds* (Cambridge, Mass.: Harvard University Press, 1997); P. Waldau, *The Specter of Speciesism: Buddhist and Christian Views of Animals* (New York: Oxford University Press, 2002); T. Page, *Buddhism and Animals* (London: Ukavis, 1999).

Chapter 4

J. I. Cabezón, *Buddhism, Sexuality, and Gender* (Albany, New York: State University of New York Press, 1992); B. Faure, *The Red Thread: Buddhist Approaches to Sexuality* (Princeton, NJ: Princeton); B. Faure, *The Power of Denial: Buddhism, Purity, and Gender* (Princeton, NJ: Princeton University Press, 2003); C. Gamage, *Buddhism and Sensuality: As Recorded in the Theravada Canon* (Illinois: Northwestern University, 1998); P. Harvey, *An Introduction to Buddhist Ethics: Foundations, Values and Issues* (Cambridge: Cambridge University Press, 2000), chapters 9–10; L. P. N. Perera, *Sexuality in Ancient India: A Study Based on the Pali Vinayapitaka* (Sri Lanka: University of Kelaniya, 1993); J. Stevens, *Lust for Enlightenment: Buddhism and Sex* (Boston: Shambhala, 1990).

Chapter 5

T. J. Bartholomeusz, *In Defence of Dharma: Just-war Ideology in Buddhist Sri Lanka* (London: Routledge Curzon, 2002); E. J. Harris, 'Buddhism and the Justification of War: A Case Study from Sri Lanka', in *Just War in Comparative Perspective*, ed. P. Robinson (Aldershot: Ashgate, 2003), pp. 93–106; I. Harris, *Buddhism and Politics in Twentieth-Century Asia* (London: Continuum, 2001); P. Harvey, *An Introduction to Buddhist Ethics: Foundations, Values and Issues* (Cambridge: Cambridge University Press, 2000), chapter 6; K. Kraft, *Inner Peace, World Peace: Essays on Buddhism and Nonviolence* (Albany, New York: State University of New York Press, 1992); D. R. Loy, 'Buddhist Reflections on the New Gulf War': *http:// www.wrinet.com/conflictforum/news/david_200303.html*; P. D. Hershock, 'From Vulnerability to Virtuosity: Buddhist Reflections on

Responding to Terrorism and Tragedy', *Journal of Buddhist Ethics*, 10 (2003): 21–38; G. D. Paige and S. Gilliatt, *Buddhism and Non-Violent Global Problem-Solving* (Honolulu: Center for Global Nonviolence Planning Project, Spark M. Matsunaga Institute for Peace, University of Hawaii Press, 1991); L. Schmithausen, 'Aspects of the Buddhist Attitude Towards War', in *Violence Denied: Violence, Non-Violence and the Rationalization of Violence in South Asian Cultural History*, ed. Jan E. M. Houben and Karel R. Van Kooij (Leiden: Brill, 1999), pp. 45–67; B. D. A. Victoria, *Zen at War* (New York and Tokyo: Weatherhill, 1997); B. D. A. Victoria, *Zen War Stories* (London: Routledge Curzon, 2003); U. Tahtinen, *Non-Violent Theories of Punishment: Indian and Western* (Delhi: Motilal Banarsidass, 1983).

Chapter 6

R. Florida, 'Buddhism and Abortion', in *Contemporary Buddhist Ethics*, ed. Damien Keown (Richmond, Surrey: Curzon Press, 2000); H. Hardacre, *Marketing the Menacing Fetus in Japan* (Berkeley, CA: University of California Press, 1997); P. Harvey, *An Introduction to Buddhist Ethics: Foundations, Values and Issues* (Cambridge: Cambridge University Press, 2000), chapter 8; Damien Keown, *Buddhism and Abortion* (London/Honolulu: Macmillan/University of Hawaii Press, 1999); Damien Keown, *Buddhism and Bioethics* (London: Palgrave, 2001); W. A. LaFleur, *Liquid Life: Abortion and Buddhism in Japan* (Princeton: Princeton University Press, 1992); A. Whittaker, *Abortion, Sin and the State in Thailand* (London: RoutledgeCurzon, 2004).

Chapter 7

C. B. Becker, 'Buddhist Views of Suicide and Euthanasia', *Philosophy East and West*, 40 (1990): 543–56; R. Florida, 'Buddhist Approaches to Euthanasia', *Studies in Religion [Sciences religieuses]*, 22 (1993): 35–47; P. Harvey, *An Introduction to Buddhist Ethics: Foundations, Values and Issues* (Cambridge: Cambridge University Press, 2000), chapter 7; Damien Keown and J. Keown, 'Karma, Killing and Caring: Buddhist and Christian Perspectives on Euthanasia', *Journal of Medical Ethics*, 21 (1995): 265–9; R. W. Perrett, 'Buddhism, Euthanasia and the

Sanctity of Life', *Journal of Medical Ethics*, 22 (1996): 309–13;
P. Ratanakul, 'To Save or Let Go: Thai Buddhist Perspectives on
Euthanasia', in *Contemporary Buddhist Ethics*, ed. Damien Keown
(Richmond, Surrey: Curzon Press, 2000).

Chapter 8

M. G. Barnhart, 'Nature, Nurture, and No-Self: Bioengineering and
Buddhist Values', *Journal of Buddhist Ethics* (*http://jbe.gold.ac.uk/7/
barnhart001.html*); E. Falls, J. D. Skeel, and W. J. Edinger, 'The Koan of
Cloning: A Buddhist Perspective on the Ethics of Human Cloning
Technology', *Second Opinion*, No. 1 (1999): 44–56 (online at *http://
www.parkridgecenter.org/Page169.html*); B. Huimin, 'Buddhist
Bioethics: The Case of Human Cloning and Embryo Stem Cell
Research', *Chung-Hwa Buddhist Journal*, 15 (2002): 457–70 (in
Chinese).

Glossary

abhidharma: 'higher Dharma', scholasticism

adveṣa: benevolence

amoha: understanding

anātman: the Buddhist doctrine of 'no self'

arāga: non-attachment

arhat: a 'worthy one' or saint who has attained nirvana

ātman: the soul or self in Hindu teachings

bardö: in Tibetan Buddhism, an intermediate state between birth and death

bodhisattva: an 'enlightenment being', a follower of Mahāyāna Buddhism

Brahma-vihāras: 'Divine Abidings', a set of four states of mind cultivated especially through meditation: loving-kindness, compassion, sympathetic joy, and equanimity

brahmin: a member of the priestly caste of Hinduism

Buddha: an 'awakened one', one who is fully enlightened and has attained nirvana

cakravartin: a 'wheel turner', a mythical ideal ruler or righteous king

dāna: generosity

Dharma: natural law

duḥkha: suffering, unsatisfactoriness

dveṣa: hatred

Jātakas: stories of the Buddha's previous lives from the Khuddaka Nikāya of the Pāli canon

karma: action, moral retribution

karuṇā: compassion

kleśa: negative disposition of character, 'vice'

kṣānti: patience

kuśala: good, wholesome, virtuous

maṇḍala: cosmic diagram or circular design illustrating Buddhist teachings

Māra: the Buddhist 'Satan'

mantra: a sound or formula having magic power

mizuko kuyō: a memorial service following an abortion in Japan

moha: delusion, ignorance

nirvana: the goal of the Buddhist path; the state of perfect enlightenment attained by Buddhas and *arhats*

pāṇa: life, breath

paṇḍaka: an effeminate homosexual man

pāramitā: one the six 'perfections', or virtues, of a bodhisattva

pāpa: evil deeds, bad karma; the opposite of *puṇya*

prajñā: insight, knowledge, wisdom

puṇya: good deeds, merit, good karma; the opposite of *pāpa*

rāga: desire, craving

samādhi: meditative trance, concentration

saṃsāra: cyclic existence

sangha: the Buddhist order of monks and nuns

śīla: morality, self-restraint

skandha: one of the five components of human nature

sūtra/sutta: a discourse of the Buddha

tṛṣṇā: desire, craving

tripiṭaka: the 'three baskets' of the Buddha's teachings, the Buddhist canon

upāya-kauśalya: 'Skilful Means', the doctrine that teachings and practice can be adapted to circumstances

Vinaya: Buddhist monastic law

Index

Expand your collection of
VERY SHORT INTRODUCTIONS

Visit the
VERY SHORT INTRODUCTIONS
Web site

www.oup.co.uk/vsi

➤ **Information** about all published titles

➤ News of **forthcoming books**

➤ **Extracts** from the books, including titles not yet published

➤ **Reviews** and views

➤ **Links** to other **web sites** and main OUP web page

➤ Information about **VSIs in translation**

➤ **Contact** the editors

➤ **Order** other **VSIs** on-line